This book explores the 'craft of use', the cultivated, ordinary and ingenious ideas and practices that promote satisfying and resourceful use of garments, presenting them as an alternative, dynamic, experiential frame with which to articulate and foster sustainability in the fashion sector.

Here Kate Fletcher provides a broad imagining of sustainability in fashion that gives attention to tending and wearing garments – favouring their use as much as their creation. She offers a diversified view of fashion beyond the market and the market's purpose and reveals fashion provision and expression in a world not dependent on continuous consumption.

Framing design and use as a single whole, the book uncovers a more contingent and time-dependent role for design in sustainability, recognising that garments, while sold as a product, are lived as a process. Drawing from stories and portrait photography that document the ways in which members of the public from across three continents use their clothes, and the work of seven international design teams seeking to amplify these use practices, the book presents a changed social narrative for fashion, borne out of ideas of satisfaction and interdependence, of action, knowledge and human agency, that glimpses fashion post-growth.

For nearly two decades Kate Fletcher's work has shaped the field of fashion and sustainability, and come to define it. She works with fashion businesses, education, non-profits and government. She is Professor of Sustainability, Design, Fashion at the University of the Arts, London, UK. This is her fourth book.

First published 2016

by Routledge
2 Park Square, Milton Park, Abingdon,
Oxon OX14 4RN

and by Routledge
711 Third Avenue, New York, NY 10017

*Routledge is an imprint of the Taylor & Francis
Group, an informa business*

© 2016 Kate Fletcher

Trademark notice: Product or corporate names
may be trademarks or registered trademarks,
and are used only for identification and
explanation without intent to infringe.

British Library Cataloguing-in-Publication Data
A catalogue record for this book is available
from the British Library

Library of Congress Cataloging-in-Publication Data
Fletcher, Kate, 1971– author.
Craft of Use: Post-Growth Fashion / Kate Fletcher.
pages, cm
Designed by Fraser Muggeridge studio.

Includes bibliographical references and index.

1. Fashion design. 2. Sustainable design. I. Title.

Printed and bound in India by Replika Press Pvt. Ltd.

TT507.F5825 2016
746.9'2--dc23
2015030690

ISBN: 978-1-138-02100-6 (hbk)
ISBN: 978-1-138-02101-3 (pbk)
ISBN: 978-1-315-64737-1 (ebk)

Craft of Use

Post-Growth Fashion

Kate Fletcher

Routledge
Taylor & Francis Group

LONDON AND NEW YORK

For Jude and Cole and for Larry and Jean,
down and up the generations

Acknowledgements

This book is created from the stories of others. To all of the nearly 500 members of the public who shared their ideas and clothing use practices with me, I extend heartfelt thanks. You teach all of us who are formally involved with the fashion sector lessons of greatness and humility.

To the *Local Wisdom* project's international network, the institutions, the lead researchers, other staff and students, huge gratitude to you all. In particular to Lynda Grose at California College of the Arts, San Francisco, USA; Timo Rissanen at Parsons the New School, New York, USA; Vibeke Riisberg at Kolding School of Design, Denmark; Hélène Day Fraser at Emily Carr University of Art and Design, Vancouver, Canada; Jo Cramer at RMIT, Melbourne, Australia, and Holly McQuillan and Jen Whitty at Massey University, Wellington, New Zealand. Nowhere does there exist a more expert and lovely group of individuals to work with to foster radical change in the fashion sector.

Thank you to the many photographers whose images of the practitioners of use bring this book alive, specifically: Kerry Dean, Paul Allister, Aliscia Young, Ellinor Stigle, Jeremy Calhoun, Tim Mitchell, Jens Christian, Paige Green, Des Moriarty, Kristin von Hirsch, Stefan Rother, Sean Michael and Fiona Bailey. Thanks also to Danai Tsouloufa for her wonderful illustrations and to Fraser Muggeridge studio for the book design, so wonderful.

Thank you to those who helped comment on early drafts of this book, in particular Katelyn, Anna, Dilys and Mathilda. You are generous, kind and wise. You 'larched', I roosted. I am very grateful.

To the wonderful team at the Centre for Sustainable Fashion, thank you for realising that both commitment and caring are essential to a changed future.

To Katelyn Toth-Fejel who worked, sailed, walked and laughed with me throughout this project, I am indebted to you a hundred times over for your industry, your brightness of spirit and your clever, curious mind.

I am grateful to The Leverhulme Trust who generously funded the research on which this book is based.

Finally, thank you to my boys and my husband for your presence, your patience and your interruptions, all of them necessary.

1
Use and Using

The Stories of Ethics of Use,
Material Resourcefulness
and Transfer of Ownership

The stories of 'ethics of use'

Brands control fashion supply chains assiduously; but
downstream, after a garment is sold, the user is in charge.
A user's subsequent actions can uphold a brand's values,
be incurious about them or defy them in a range of
direct or subtle ways. When it happens, subversion comes
in many forms: the protestations of a blog, the cutting
and reworking of scissors and thread, or the attitude
with which a garment is worn, upending the worldview
of the corporation that made it.

Long life as a political tool

I got this when I first went to New York in 1986. It's an old jumper … early purchase and I've had it ever since. It's just from a shop out there 'J Crew' which probably, in itself, isn't ethical, but just because I've kept it all this time, I've forced them into it.

London, UK, 2010

Open imperfect

I'm wearing an outfit that was made for me by a man
in Chinatown. So one day I was rushing to my medical
appointment for my green card and I glanced to the right,
and there was this beautiful old Chinese man approaching
me, in a beautiful shirt. And I said to him, 'Wow, I love your
shirt, it is so beautiful'. And then he said to me 'I made it,
I made that shirt'.

   And then I said, 'Oh wow, do you make clothes?'. He couldn't
speak English very well so our conversation didn't really go
anywhere, but I said, 'Do you have a shop or are you somewhere

or can I meet you somewhere?' because he said he had more clothes. We couldn't figure it out somehow and then he said, 'come and follow me'. So I followed him ... he had a little alley that was locked off by a fence. So he opened it and put his cart and his bicycle in there.

Then he took off his shirt and he gave it to me. And then I said, 'can I give you money for it?' but he said, 'No, no, it's fine'. And then I said 'I want to give you some money for it', because I could also see he was not a wealthy person. So I gave him some money and then he said, 'shall I make clothes for you?'. I said 'Yes, please'. So we exchanged telephone numbers.

So when we meet up again he had made new clothes for me, and he had made a series so I could kind of pick clothes. He made his shirt in smaller versions for me and he made these pants for me, which are quite extraordinary, I think. And they have a lot of details (laughs). He is not a perfect sewer at all, which I love, but there is some kind of spontaneity in his compositions ... he put elastic as the fly placket.

... They are all [made from] upholstery fabric sample books, and here you have the holes still ... [from where they were bolted] in the corner? (laughs) ... I ended up with eight pieces, something like that. And I think I wear three pieces quite regularly.

This was ... I think in the late spring last year. It just touched me. He was so beautiful, and of course he also needed the money, I understood that, but I liked the way that he didn't sew so perfectly. I wish I could have this unskilled quality in my own clothes. I'm a designer, so I make clothes, and I always look for this quality. Where there's a sense of openness and spontaneity.

I [also] like sewing [with] skill ... I designed good [within] in the [commercial fashion] system ... so I also designed really finished clothes. Now I hand make clothes so I always look for that more spontaneous coming together of things. That is not restricted within the habituations of our thinking about clothes. I like things that feel free and that have a certain awareness about them.

For me it's very important that clothes are not a shield. I want to feel open to the world and I want to feel fluid in relation to the world. I don't want to feel harnessed in relation to the world [and adhering to the aesthetics of the commercial fashion industry]. So for me I always look for clothes that have this kind of opening somehow ... the kind of unexpected or unconditioned something ...

New York City, USA, 2013

Buy nothing

I'm trying not to buy anything, at all. I have a house full
of stuff. I have forty odd pairs of shoes, it's ridiculous.
And everything I go for I mean I have to ask that question
in the shop, I actually have to ask myself if it's stuff that
I already have.

Dublin, Ireland, 2012

Utility cashmere

This is a coat that my grandfather purchased at the department store Lord and Tailor, in New York City in 1957. And it is made of long staple royal imperial cashmere.

My grandfather wore it to John F. Kennedy's inauguration. And stood out in the cold, to watch John F. Kennedy be sworn in as president of the United States. And then my father wore it, thirty, forty, almost fifty years later, to president Obama's inauguration and stood out in the cold and watched it. So it doesn't fit me … but I'm sure as I age, I will fill it out, as we all do …

It was seen as an investment piece of course. And you had few of them … He was a financially successful man, but he opened up his car with pliers … he just believed in utility …

Vancouver, Canada, 2013

Introduction

For more than five years I have been gathering stories and images
from the public, like those above, exploring how people use clothes.
I started because of an insistent belief that the use of fashion matters.
And I continued as my understanding of the practices of garment use
– and the ideas, skills and capabilities they invoke – began to grow into
a new vision for the fashion sector in the era of resource scarcity, climate
change and consumerism. This new view, and the stories of which it
is a part, make up this book. At its heart it proposes a very simple idea
of change: to give attention to tending and wearing garments; to favour
their use as much as their creation. And in so doing to adopt a more
ecological idea of fashion that recognises what happens beyond design
and production as rich, powerful, valuable.

   Pay attention to the practices of use, and we pay attention to
fashion in larger contexts: the 'life world' of people who wear clothes,
their actions, their ideas, how they configure materials, how their
choices combine to affect the whole. Notice the context of use and
we acknowledge fashion values and actions that fall outside the normal
terms of reference of the market, we exercise our fashion intelligence
in a broader field. Hone our attention on using garments and we may
start to question the legitimacy of the assumption, firmly lodged in
global understandings of success and development, that continuous
growth in sales is essential, that more is better, that it leads to life.

   These pages feature and reference much of the material gathered
by the *Local Wisdom* project,[1] research that both documented how
people use clothes with stories and portrait photography and explored
ways in which design practice might develop with exposure to ideas
and practices of use. The recording process spanned 16 locations
in nine countries across three continents, and collected almost 500
tales of practices of garment use. The design work took place in seven
universities and over 80 design projects (of various sizes and formats)
were completed. They reveal a set of little noticed or prized practical
skills, knowledge and ideas associated with using clothes; practices
which quickly became dubbed the 'craft of use'.

   In the course of talking to people about how they use garments,
it soon became apparent that the lens of use changes our ideas about

fashion provision and experience with unprecedented and profound effects. For what the craft of use represents is compelling possibilities and practicalities for fashion mainly within the clothes we already have. Using things is not dependent on producing and consuming more, and yet it fulfils many of the needs we try to meet when we buy new goods. It takes its bearings from the practices and ideas of tending and wearing, in the context of real lives. It is a diversified view of fashion beyond the market and the market's purpose, trading in the economies of time, creativity and community. Quietly–practically– directly, a focus on the practices of use is a focus on fashion not driven by the exigencies and resource impacts of rising consumption alone. It is an unnerving, refreshing and revolutionary view: a glimpse of fashion provision and expression beyond consumerism.

That such a view doesn't fit within conventional industry-sponsored ideas of change, that it doesn't reinforce an absolute loyalty to a consumerist way of life on which corporate power depends, gives the craft of use rare and disruptive influence. I should say at the outset that this book is an eclectic gathering of work in this area, a collection of starting points, and it is essential that it is adapted, improved – for these ideas hold little power without input and extension. A bold voice in this bigger conversation is yours; my fellow user, designer, producer of clothes. For the message of these pages exists only in relation to what happens in your business context, your home, your wardrobe, your life. What I have come to realise is that to use is to act, to forge a more engaged future of our own choosing and, in so doing, to provide us with an opportunity to develop the capacity and skills to navigate our own route not just through our fashion choices, but also through life. It is as the Spanish proverb so deftly states, 'There is no path. Paths are made by walking'. We are the makers of alternative routes. The craft of use is a stance and avenue of action for a different future.

Paths of use

Happily our ways are already criss-crossed with many paths of use. Some of them are in this book. The stories that run through these pages are often chaotic, and I let their unruliness have free rein here. I offer them up as a carnival of ideas, actions, relationships and material consequences, a fiesta of on-going use of fashion over time. Here and counter to the norm, fashion attention is lavished upon what happens *beyond* the point of purchase, not before it. Use practices are celebrated as an interdependent, if underground, part of the fashion system and one of influence: our experiences of products, like garments, *as we use them* deeply affect our satisfaction with them.[2]

These paths of use also have other characteristics. Let's be clear, using garments draws down resources, however the rates of material flows associated with use practices are often low. Little in the way of materials (from the stories, mainly thread, yarn, an occasional zip) and money (beyond the original purchase) is needed to use clothes over and again. For maintaining what we have, keeping garments in active use can involve something as simple as approaching a piece with attention and imagination. There is also some 'inconspicuous consumption'[3] of resources involved in on-going use, including that associated with laundering garments. Yet, perhaps because use practices are enabled by, but not rooted in industry and commodity products, perhaps because they are distanced from the drivers of economic growth, they are often resource effective over time.

The activities embedded within the paths of use are also human-scale. They are pragmatic and within the realm and reach of us all. They cast their narrators as practitioners, craftsmen and women, of use. They are fashion practitioners not because they are designing a new collection, but because they are using what they have with dedication and passion. They show insights, ideas and new ways of wearing and thinking about clothes that build towards a satisfaction with what people already have. They draw on well-established practices of thrift, of domestic provisioning, of care for others, on the gift economy, on the informal channels through which clothes pass between friends and family. They stretch resources qualitatively and quantitatively, making them go further, appreciating them in greater detail, infusing them with human warmth and memory, folding them into others' lives. This gives satisfaction: aesthetic pleasure, social regard, an ethical concern for others, the taking of responsibility for material effects.

The paths of use, the skills and competencies, the ideas and actions are ageless, as old as clothing itself. But to make use itself the narrative is new. Many of the elements that I draw upon in these pages will already be familiar to you, but the practices and context of use link things together in a novel way. The craft of use is replete with material and ideological manipulation of garments and the agency to produce the world differently. On-going use is an affront to the consumer society, a slur on throwaway culture. It is fashion in a space where we choose 'to want what one has'[4] and one where we revel in the power, imagination and possibility that it offers. American environmentalist Bill McKibben describes the change in priorities thus: 'After a long period of frenetic growth, we're suddenly older. Old, even. And old people worry less about getting more; they care more about hanging on to what they have, or losing it as slowly as possible ... your goal becomes to husband that wealth'.[5]

Planetary boundaries

The urgent need to engage systemically with environmental, social and economic considerations is now formally and globally recognised.[6] In 2009, a comprehensive piece of research led by Sweden's Stockholm Resilience Centre gave definition to the speed and scale of change required.[7] The work captures the world as a giant ecosystem with a sensitive biosphere with an astonishingly complex array of inter-related and unpredictable fluctuations stimulated by people and their actions. It identified nine planetary boundaries as critical to health and stability of Earth systems; all of which were under threat from human activity. Alarmingly, at least three planetary boundaries have already been crossed: human intervention in nitrogen cycles, biodiversity loss and climate change. Each transgression is serious in its own right; however, because changes in earth systems are non-linear, their potential effects include the dramatic and asymmetrical impact upon other boundaries, threatening the collapse of the larger systems. Indeed such is the significance of the influence of human activity on the earth's atmosphere, that a new geological epoch has been constituted to name our human-changed world, *the anthropocene*. The extent and effects of human influence on the health of global ecosystems are without precedent. This is the context in which all people, all industrial sectors, now sit.

'Alarmingly, at least three planetary boundaries have already been crossed'

The impacts of fashion production and culture

Since the early years of the 1990s, the impact of both fashion production and fashion culture on ecological and social systems has been increasingly identified. Today it is estimated that clothing represents 5% to 10% of environmental impacts generated across the 25 nations of the European Union.[8] Further it is thought that 25% of chemicals produced worldwide are used for textiles[9] and 20% of global industrial water pollution comes from textile dyeing and finishing.[10] About 4% of the total of each UK citizen's water use is considered to result from use of cotton fabric alone.[11] An estimated 60 billion kg of textiles and footwear are lost (burned or landfilled) every year in the world.[12] At the same time worker abuses in supply chains continue and are symbolised by the horror of the Rana Plaza factory collapse in Bangladesh in 2013 where more than 1100 garment workers lost their lives. Moreover, as a culture, fashion is bound up with systems of economic growth and consumerism which contribute to high levels – and an ever-increasing pace – of individualized consumption. Fashion is readily characterised as the poster-industry of consumerist materialism; as frivolous, superficial and evanescent; a sector that delivers change without development. It is shaped by the superfluity of mass production and unlimited consumption; an industry linked to abysmal abuses of workers' rights, resource intensive and polluting supply chains, waste generation, ideas predicated on the image, on status competition and ownership, on individualised success.

Fashion and the challenge of sustainability

Fashion is also a space at the heart of contemporary culture, and one that fuses provision of livelihoods, creative expression, social processes, fundamental human needs and personal pleasure. Such forces demand we embrace fashion for the cultural force that it is, in full acknowledgment of its negative effects, not simply oppose it. Over the last two decades, there have been many attempts to increase the resource efficiency of the fashion sector. These have resulted in a range of products which make use of lower impact materials

and processes;[13] more resource efficient more transparent production
chains;[14] home laundering practices which use less energy and water;[15]
and new and more varied opportunities to donate and reuse garments
at the end of a first life.[16] Further initiatives around green chemistry,
cleaner production and co-ordination and communication of
these improvements through corporate social responsibility (CSR)
programmes, are now widespread and a tacit requirement of being
in business. Moreover cross-industry sustainability initiatives, like
the Sustainable Apparel Coalition,[17] are working to increase the
environmental efficiency of the baseline operating standards of
the sector as a whole in an effort to reduce all production impact.

Yet evidence suggests that, despite these substantial efforts, the
net impact of the sector has not reduced.[18] Resource savings brought
by efficiency drives have, in the same period that improvements have
been introduced, been outstripped by higher rates of consumption of
clothes, increasing the impact of the system at large. Viewed as a whole,
things have got worse, not better. For example, efficiency improvements
have reduced resource use by 30% per unit in 2010 as compared
with 1980, yet sales of new garments more than doubled between 1977
and 2007; [19] and in 2013, the last year for which figures were available,
they grew by 8.9% to US$460 billion.[20] Fashion companies make and
sell increasingly more units because that is the business model they
are working in. Continuous growth in sales of clothing is their goal.
Increasing the throughput of materials is their mechanism. Yet this
is spectacularly detrimental: continuous expansion of use of materials
is fundamentally at odds with the finite nature of the resource base.
The cumulative effects of consumption are not recognised because
no one is in charge of the whole. Parts of systems are worked on
in isolation, but how those parts work together is unknown.

Categorically we need a different approach. Industry and its systems
are designed for efficiency. New ideas emerging from existing systems
will always be efficiency-focused, incremental, predictable. We need to
break free from existing ways of thinking and address, without timidity,
that which governs the sustainability potential of the fashion sector:
the scale, pace and summative character of growth and consumption.

Thus the project at stake, in fashion as in many other sectors,
is one about the goals, rules, foundational patterns and models

that shape the actions of the sector as a whole – and society beyond. We need to develop imaginative understanding of how our relationship with growth and consumerism has brought us to this place. We also need a vital, inquisitive freedom to think anew about other ways of doing things. To move towards fashion sustainability, such ways of knowing will have to be distributed widely. This is the craft of use's territory. To choose what we are and what we do with clothes daily is to have the power to alter the fashion system. The confining and captivating parts of our fashion experiences become a new view on what is possible. To wit, tales of 'material resourcefulness' with fashion, collected from the public, become tiny lessons of change.

The stories of 'material resourcefulness'

Garments are fusions of materials and energy brought
to the body in myriad configurations, yet the dominant
force in fashion, consumerism, tends to value only a
narrow spectrum of fashion activity. The practices of
material resourcefulness broaden this view and show
a burgeoning testing ground of an alternative flow
of fibre, fabric and product.

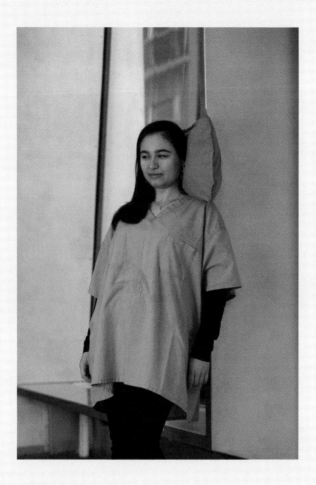

Repurpose everything

I went to my aunt's house over Christmas break and I
noticed that the pillowcase that was on my cousin's bed
looked a lot like my dad's old hospital uniform ... she
repurposes everything.

   My favourite story about her is that when my older cousin
moved out of the house, she wanted to re-purpose his bedroom,
to make a living space. So, instead of taking his old bed
out and putting a sofa in, she cut his mattress in half. That's
literally what she did (laughs) ... It's not like in Mexico they
have less. They have a very special cultural habit to not throw
things out.

New York City, USA, 2013

Memory scarf

I worked in Nigeria in the late 1970s and I came back and
I got a job in the north of England and it was very cold
and my mother was very worried about me so she knitted
me this scarf obviously out of old bits of wool that she
had got left over from other garments ... I know, for
example, the original garments that this wool came from.
I'm colour blind by the way ... so is this orange? Yes that
came out of a sort of sleeveless pullover that she knitted
for me. The blue was a jersey that she knitted for my
sister I remember ...

Berlin, Germany, 2010

Whipped it up

My T-shirt, I made the other morning before I left the house to go do my errands; I just bought a bunch of new fabric to sew some new wardrobe stuff. And I just whipped it up, um pretty quick. After I made it I just wore it day and night. I slept in it and just kept wearing it for like days, probably like four days and I haven't stained it yet which is a miracle for a white T-shirt.

San Francisco, USA, 2012

Reuse

The yarn for this jacket is from a house guest of mine,
'Chester' a chow dog. One day I was brushing him and
his down hair was coming away, and I was thinking, this
is a waste. So I got on the phone to my friend Valerie, a
spinner, and I said, 'do you do dog?' 'Of course!' she said,
'I can do anything!' So the discussion went on, see, she
explained to me how to collect and store the hair until
I could get it to her. And then Valerie looked at it and saw
that the staple was too short to spin on its own, so she blended
it with Tussah silk. You don't need a fancy pattern because
the yarn is beautiful in its own right, furry down texture
with glints of silk.

Bollington, UK, 2009

Utilise it all

Working in the fashion industry, I usually run across a lot
of sample fabrics or left over remnants … so I always try
to utilise them …

   I had this piece of leather for many years and I finally
thought that I would play around with it. This was just a skin.
So I started to bleach it and I noticed that one side was solid
and the other side got bleached so I thought let me wash it.
I put it in the washing machine and then the dryer and it got
really nice and this is how it came out. And so now I have this
really nice – it almost looks like a print so I thought of making
a skirt in one piece without any zippers. So I pieced it together.
You can see where – there's no side seam. I pieced it together
and I made like a little pleat for closure and I made a makeshift
dart over here. I used every little piece of it the skin.

New York City, USA, 2013

Step-in dress

I'm wearing a local designer's – I guess it's a one of a kind –
dress. She makes everything to order and it's made out of
a 1950s' floral print tablecloth. And you step into it, she calls
them step-in dresses and it just zips up and you're ready to go.

San Francisco, USA, 2012

Societal values

My jewellery is made entirely with recycled materials which
I've worked with for 23 years, [starting] when working with
like recycled materials and trash was somewhat embarrassing.
Most of my work is made out of recycled tin cans … I feel
like the packaging of our consumer society reflects the values
of our society.

San Francisco, USA, 2011

Quilt coat

This coat is made of an old quilt. It's a quilt that my grandmother was going to throw away ... it was tattered and it has been in the wash with something black and gotten this black tint to it. So I made it into a coat. It's zero waste, none of the quilt was wasted. The extra pieces, the selvedges were actually sewn into this panel right here so ... and it got a hood, which it wasn't initially going to have. It basically became a princess seamed coat instead of just the normal coat that I was going to make.

And then the arms got this treatment because I had to fit the fabric pieces into the quilt.

New York City, USA, 2013

Post-growth economics

More than 40 years ago Gregory Bateson[21] described the need for a shift from a mentality of 'survival of the fittest' to 'survival of organisms plus environment' – a shift that argued that an ecological struggle for survival is taking place in the domain of ideas. It is increasingly acknowledged, including in industry, that fashion and sustainability needs ecologically 'good' ideas to evolve its practice in ways other than the growth and consumption model that dominates conceptions of fashion today.

An economic conversation dominated by continuous growth fails to take account of our understanding of what motivates and enriches people, and the 'safe operating space for humanity' that we might carefully carve out within planetary boundaries.[22] A different vision of economics is called for, where economies grow less or very differently, one that develops a more integrated picture of social and material aspects to facilitate holistic health. Such a shift is also essential for human well-being. Beyond the point at which basic needs are met, a growth in levels of consumption adds little to well-being, and even undermines it.[23] Not only that, but a materialistic mindset has been shown to work against two hallmarks of psychological health and high quality of life, closer interpersonal relationships and connection with others.[24]

Economic historian, Avner Offer, suggests that one route to holistic health is found in actively choosing not to maximise levels of consumption, but to pace it back to the level of best satisfaction, to keep the flow of rewards under control. He pithily lays it out: 'Affluence has liberated people; though more moderate affluence would have sufficed'.[25] The message is simple; we can thrive with less, we can choose not to burst through constraints and still be happy.[26] Such a choice – if we can carry it through – has scope to generate what Tim Jackson calls a 'double dividend',[27] reducing levels of consumption to benefit both individual welfare and collective environment quality. It even offers the prospect of exposing a 'foundational delusion of the consumer society': 'that getting without giving (beyond monetarily) is possible',[28] an idea that suggests that our lives are part of a bigger relational whole, acknowledged when we give as well as take.

The ideas underpinning this changed economic conversation draw
on the work of an increasingly vocal body of commentators looking to
formulate alternative economic structures and social practices designed
to foster prosperity without growth.[29] Here the goal is to define and
describe economic activity by ecological limits, to reverse the view
within standard economics that an economy is an isolated system in
which exchange value circulates between firms and households, an
isolated system that has no environment and no constraints. By contrast,
in 'post-growth' or 'steady-state' economics, 'the economy is an open
subsystem of a finite and nongrowing ecosystem ... that must itself
at some point also become nongrowing'.[30] According to World Bank
economist Herman Daly, such a system is far from static or turgid,
'The steady-state economy can develop qualitatively but does not
grow in quantitative scale'[31] – knowledge, time, goodness, community,
creativity, ethical codes, the allocation of resources are not held constant.
Design/technology gets an explicit mention, 'Not only is [its] quality
free to evolve, but its development is positively encouraged'.[32] Daly
goes on, 'The end of physical accretion is not the end of progress.
It is more a precondition for future progress, in the sense of qualitative
improvement.'[33] Such an economy taps into neglected assets, with wealth
attained by mobilising and transforming social and ecological 'economies'
as much as materials.[34] By taking the emphasis off economic markets we
open up opportunities for new, less consumerist forms of social language
and stories to emerge.

Daly is clear that a change in our approach to growth is radical,
a paradigm shift, a change in the 'preanalytic vision' we bring to the
problem, necessary because the current approach is itself the cause of
our suffering. Unless we move our thinking and practice outside the
context of growth, the problems of unsustainability, including in the
fashion sector, will remain fundamentally insoluble. He argues instead for
a gestalt switch towards a different future, and one in which we 'shift the
incentives towards ecological adaptation, that is to accept natural limits to
the size and dominion of the human household, to concentrate on moral
growth and qualitative improvement'.[35] Here the craft of use finds a
home within a context of resource scarcity and its productive constraints.
It is as Anni Albers notes: 'Acceptance of limitations, as a framework
rather than as a hindrance, is always proof of a productive mind'.[36]

The craft of use and stories of our times

The use of fashion plays a part in many important stories of our time. It is woven into the urgent need to live differently within global planetary boundaries. It is a running stitch concerned with the welfare of others. Use tangles with the dominance of market thinking and economic growth and the inability of efficiency improvements to outrun the negative effects of increasing consumption. It is knitted together with material dimensions of well-being, 'enoughness', mindfulness and commitment strategies for the future. It is wound around threads of everyday behaviours and relationships and pragmatic rather than rationalist thinking as a basis for how we build society. It is spun out of narratives of change that see sustainability as a political not just a technical challenge.

Use imagines sustainability as coming not from separate component parts, but from synthesis, from the joy and love of fashion and from clothes in the context of cluttered, unpredictable real lives. Its stories are those of engagement, satisfaction, responsibility, capabilities, material reverence, vital materialism, skilled fingers, tacit knowledge, of acting as if 'stuff' is properly ours. And at the same time it is also about authenticity and personal completeness by having less dependency on material context, a shift in orientation from having to being. And yet engaging with the use of fashion is also a very simple story. It is a story about how we want to live – and thrive – how we engage with the shirts on our backs, with culture and with ecological systems in an unpredictable, changing world. It can be as simple as gifting a garment to someone else.

The stories of 'transfer of ownership'

Giving a garment to someone else is sometimes a
straightforward and spontaneous act. At other times
a transfer of ownership is more circuitous. Periods
of overlapping ownership often intensify resource
use and stud a garment's story with memories.

Never too old

Before I was home last, my 93-year-old – 94 at the end of next week – mom was going through stuff, trying to clear out her house ... This little leopard skin dress, she made when she was 80 and wore it all the time and loved it. And she decided to get rid of it ... I wear it loose or with this belt that she wore with it.

Marin City, USA, 2012

Rather not wear it than lose it

So I am wearing my dad's air force jacket. He was in the
US army for a good part of his young life and had a bunch
of uniform that was decommissioned and given to him
when he left and when I moved to Wellington it was colder
than I was expecting and I didn't really have a coat ... but
he calls me every couple of weeks, to check up on me but
mostly to check up on his jacket. He's like, 'you still got it?'
    I lent it out once and he was so angry! He said, 'oh how's
my jacket doing?' And I said, 'Ahh I lent it out to Cami to get
home when it was raining out'. And he was like, 'you did what?'
'Can you trust this boy, do you know who he is? Do you know
where it is, have you got it back yet?' And so he loves it to pieces
so I try and take good care of it. But it's kind of ironic because
it was always a work jacket for him. So it's covered in bits of
paint. It's coming apart at the seams ... but I like how it's just
much too big for me and the pockets are everywhere ... It's
my one good thick coat but if I know that I'm going to go
somewhere where I might need to take it off and put it down
I'd rather wear a bunch of jerseys and cardigans and my thin
coat instead just because if I lost this one I would be murdered
and also really sad that it was gone.

Wellington, New Zealand, 2013

Energy of a grandmother

This jacket which my grandmother sewed when she was young.
And I got a lot of her clothes … it's very good quality and this
one I'm very glad of, it's very nice. I think, like, one fifth of my
clothes are actually from my grandmother. She just had a lot
of energy and she was just sewing a lot so yeah so I got a lot
of clothes from her …

Kolding, Denmark, 2012

Noreen

This blazer is my best friend's, her grandmother Noreen's
blazer ... My friend loves it but it doesn't suit her style and
she wants it to live on, so she thought of me and she passed
it down to me so I am sort of keeping it on behalf of her family
as an heirloom. So it's very important for me to take super
good care of it. And I only wear it if I am feeling very fancy.

I never met Noreen. No. I don't have connection to
specifically with her. But I do with my friend and I feel like
I am wearing it for her in a way. I feel ... a responsibility.
It's borrowed. It's lent. It's not mine. Yet everything [else]
that I own, I don't feel connected to any of it ... they don't ...
um ... they don't seem to have ... weight.

Vancouver, Canada, 2013

Inherited

This is a dressing gown, which is actually quite ugly. I don't
like the colours at all. It's sort of purplish and green. They don't
fit in with my flat or with my bathroom, but it was my father's.
I inherited it. I put it on every morning after I've had a shower.
And somebody said that it might also have to do with a warm
feeling of security; that it feels almost like an embrace.
Normally I've got skulls in my flat.

Berlin, Germany, 2010

Familial lending library

The dress was my aunt's … I think she probably bought
it in the 80s. And she gave it to me a couple of years ago.
And I shortened the hem and changed the neckline. But
in her basement there is basically a closet she has kept for
me and my sister. And so, she really liked fashion, in the 80s
and 90s … a little kind of library of clothing. She likes for
us to just go and take whatever we want.

Vancouver, Canada, 2013

Mother–sister–sister

This skirt was originally my mother's. She bought it when she was travelling in her early twenties. She had it in her wardrobe for a long time, and at one point my sister spied it and liked it very much. And my mother gave it to my sister and my sister moved to New York City and she brought it with her. And then when I moved to New York City and since slowly it's kind of migrated to my wardrobe. It kind of spanned, or moved through three people's wardrobes, and two people that wear it very regularly, sharing it, I guess.

New York City, USA, 2013

Grandmother's gifts

I've brought three belts … This belt was from a friend …
and this one … I don't remember any more, but it maybe
that this came either from my grandmother or from my
neighbour. My grandmother always collects pieces of
clothing from relatives and then my sister and I, we chose
what we like. That belt is also from my grandmother,
I think either from a cousin or from an acquaintance.

Berlin, Germany, 2010

Fit depends

This shirt, it was given by this special friend who was leaving
London and loved this shirt but it didn't fit him very well
so he didn't want to take it with him, so he gave it to me.
The shirt was too big for him I think and it is much too
big for me, but I think it fits me well so we were both happy.

London, UK, 2012

Pick me up

This is a bed jacket that my mother let me wear when I really
wasn't feeling well as a young kid and when I had to stay in
bed … It was given to my mother by her mother for the same
reasons, and her mother I think is the one who bought it …

    My mother, she'd pull [it] out and her jewellery box and
allow me to wear it, to dress up in it and try her rings on,
rather than think about how ill I was feeling.

Dublin, Ireland, 2012

Faded style

My dad has never thrown anything away so he's been keeping
lots of old T–shirts and woollen sweaters from the 70s and 80s.
And me and my sister just love them. We've borrowed them
or just took them over. The T-shirt and woollen cardigan are
my dad's. I think maybe the cardigan might even have belonged
to my grandmother before him ...

He hasn't bought many of new clothes the last twenty years
or so and the specific style he had when he was young, I'd say
has now faded away now ... He's mostly a quiet man staying
at home so he doesn't attend many social activities. So what
he wears is, I guess, mostly for himself now. But it was different
of course when he was younger.

Oslo, Norway, 2012

House of treasure

I am from a big house on a farm and we just find things around
the house from my parents and my grandparents and think
'oh something new'... Between the generations, they don't
[throw] anything out. I found this top and trousers there.
These trousers I used when I was about twelve almost every
day at school. I didn't wash them so much but then I got
new trousers so I put them away for a time, and maybe one or
two years later I found them again and then I used them every
day for about three years. And I really mean every day. I wear
clothes from both from my mum and my grandma. When I
was a little girl I always found clothes in the house and still
today I can find things: 'Oh I haven't seen it before!' But it's
not a very big house but maybe it's a house with a lot of things.

Oslo, Norway, 2012

Russian style

This is a skirt my grandmother gave it to me. She's from Russia so she made it herself, like, thirty years ago or so. It's actually too big … I just wear it with a belt … She said I could, like, shorten it but I'm too lazy. She said it's so cool and she sees a lot of people with this fabric. She's, like, always looking around and then in her own closet to see what she could give me.

Berlin, Germany, 2010

The *Local Wisdom* project

The business case for environmental and social responsibility and its industrial context has dominated ideas about fashion and sustainability for more than two decades, directing our ambitions for it and what it means to know about the field. But this is only part of the story; other ways of knowing about fashion and sustainability are possible. In the course of a few conversations a decade ago, I realised that many of us, as part of our daily lives, are already adept at using things fully and with pleasure. Indeed, the things that we are and do as we tend and wear clothes is an essential, contingent, unstructured part of the sustainability activity. I wanted to give these practices time and attention and to see if they might contain the power of insight into alternative courses of action. Would they speak out about the limits and potential of the material world and our capabilities as human beings?

And so began a journey into fashion use practices that drew for inspiration on the Indian tradition of *Shodh Yatra* (literally 'local wisdom'), a walk or crossing through a place, where a search for knowledge, creativity and innovation begins with regular folk, everyday actions at the grassroots. The 'bottom–up' approach is essential, for the practices of use are finessed in the 'business' of life, not that of high street or the quarterly report. They are shaped by all of us who wear clothes.

Fittingly perhaps, *Local Wisdom* started out very small – as two one-day 'community photoshoots' in old textile towns in England. The process was simple – we hired a space, often a community hall, set up a camera, light reflectors and tape recorder, and invited the public to come along and share the stories of how they use their clothes and have their portrait taken wearing their pieces. Each photoshoot was advertised widely in the locale: community newspapers, local radio, social media, adverts in newsagents' windows, and I hoped to draw in people including those who had perhaps worked with fibre and fabric in the town, whose knowledge of cloth and clothes was already extensive, a knowledge that I thought might also extend to a sensibility around the practices of use. I'm not sure we ever got any of these people to come. But what we did get were stories and images from a cross section of people that pointed to ideas, skills and actions associated with clothes that are almost never discussed. Use is hidden from view. It is not admired. I took part in hours of conversations (and listened again as I reviewed them later on tape) in which it was obvious that it's often hard to bring to mind what our experiences of using things actually are; that we struggle even to find the words to describe what goes on as we tend and care for and wear our clothes (tellingly, perhaps, we encounter no such difficulties when we talk about the experience of buying things). And yet, as at set of activities the practices of use satisfy our needs, stretch our imaginations and finesse our skills of material engagement with the world.

Local Wisdom 'community photoshoots'

Research methods

Drawing upon ethnographic research methods and photography, the *Local Wisdom* project, based in the Centre for Sustainable Fashion at London College of Fashion, grew to include a core of six other international academic partners: California College of the Arts, San Francisco, USA; Parsons the New School, New York, USA; Design School Kolding, Denmark; Emily Carr University of Art and Design, Vancouver, Canada; RMIT, Melbourne, Australia; and Massey University, Wellington, New Zealand; and in the course of five years visited 16 different locations. Using grounded theory methods, the stories and images were categorised into themes that emerged from the recordings themselves and then, in a new phase of work, they became folded into a design research process that set out to explore the ways in which the use practices of the public could be adapted, amplified, integrated into current activities, in order to increase their uptake. This last phase of design practice took place in seven venues in three continents, all characterised by high levels of fashion consumption: Europe, North America and Australasia. The project's ambition was to design to explore use of clothes in countries that arguably need to make the biggest change to their consumption patterns. That is, to increase usership in places where ownership is the dominant fashion experience, to connect fashion as creation to the unpredictable world of fashion as use. Many of the project's findings have found their way into these pages.

A word on terminology

Throughout this book I use the term the 'craft of use' to describe those actions and ideas associated with using garments that are resourceful, pleasurable and cultivated. Most of us are familiar with – and highly prize – the craft or expert skill of making things, like garments. We value the expert's touch honed over years of training and a process of constant refinement of technique and concept necessary to create superior pieces. I see similar practices alive in using garments. They also involve skill, ingenuity and require practice to perfect them. The craft of use is an expression both of these techniques and also their potential: to promote self-reliance and a more satisfying and engaged use of resources. It seems that the 'craft' in craft of use aligns with the contemporary discourse of craftivism in that politically engaged craft communities shares an imperative to challenge dominant economies and, 'value the radical approach of a particular craft activity rather than its finished end product'.[37]

Ways to read this book

This book has been designed to be read and rifled through in many ways. The portrait shots and stories gathered from the *Local Wisdom* interviews offer one obvious reading path. Clustered into themes, contextualised by a paragraph of introduction and interspersed throughout the book, it is possible to navigate between them, reading them alone. They make for a lookbook of fashion action that comprehends the world on its own terms. They make for serious reading, but they are also warm and sunlit. There is a lot of laughter in the stories, much revelry and irreverence.

This book is organised in seven chapters, each telling different stories about the practices of using fashion as part of designing sustainability futures. The chapters have distinct themes and can be read in any order, though some build more directly on each other. The early chapters seek to offer context and the later ones deal more with specific qualities of the craft of use. Chapter 2 more closely examines the influence of consumer culture on fashion and its sustainability effects, arguing for an essential broadening of our ideas and expectations of fashion to include the context of its use and, by extension, the context of the bigger world on which we depend. Chapter 3 explores the notion of fashion as process not product, framing garments within people's lives through time. Chapter 4 investigates the materiality of fashion within the practices of garment use, drawing upon notions such as 'true' materialism and an ethic of care that combines material culture with people. Building on this theme of relational importance between fashion and use, Chapter 5 looks at durability and its relationship with enduring use and finds that durability is a product of nurture not nature. Chapter 6 delves into capabilities and agency, exploring the craft of use as what we have in combination with what we are and do. Chapter 7 draws together the key threads of the preceding chapters together, offering the craft of use as the beginnings of a way of engaging with fashion beyond growth.

Each of the chapters that follow this one opens with photographs made by Kerry Dean[38] together with Alex McIntosh from London College of Fashion as part of the creative research practice that formed part of the *Local Wisdom* project. The images were created to respond to some of the *Local Wisdom* stories and to extend the key ideas of the craft of use in conversation with the visual language of fashion photography. Visual imagery associated with ideas, activities and artefacts of use of clothes is undeveloped, and in the shoot we endeavoured to change this a little. All the chapter-opening images were shot on polaroid film – a high skill process itself – some using multiple exposures, to hint at the passing of time, to show clothes in the setting of life. The aim in all of the shots was to strike a balance of foreground and background, to see both garment and context, to avoid dissociations between subject–object, body–spirit, humans–nature. The pieces worn in the photographs were a mix of things that we already owned or had borrowed. They, and their life worlds, are part of the texture of the shots, all taken in Highgate Woods in London; our 'manor', our context.

The typeface of this book also deserves special mention. It is created from a combination of ten popular serif fonts, each character selected from the ten font families at random and presented as a constantly changing, evolving script. An integrated part of the book's graphic design by Fraser Muggeridge studio,[39] the font extends the book's themes, and is an expression of possibility, of novelty with the things already available to us. It is maverick, imaginative, resilient; it is a little wonky, with a different rhythm and cadence that draws you in. It is the craft of use.

2

Consumerism, Sustainability and Fashion

The Stories of Alternative Dress Codes, Mixed Use and Skills of Resourcefulness

The bond between fashion and high volume material consumption can seem inexorable. And the ways in which we think about and practically tend and wear our garments – our fashion use practices – are intensely coloured by this dynamic; suffused with the priorities and power relations of capitalism and the market. Today, the language and expression of consumer culture in our experience of fashion is so overriding that we hardly notice it. In the collective cultural consciousness of much of the rich global North, fashion *is* novelty, consumption, materialism, commercialisation and marketing. It is buying high street and high end. It is watching, shopping, purchasing, having. The prevailing consumerist fashion style and story appears 'natural' to our way of thinking and behaviour: it is normal to access and engage with fashion primarily by exchanging money for product; it is expected that these same products will look dated and stylistically incongruous in six months; it is usual to discard rather than repair. To the extent that a belief in fashion-as-consumption dominates our experience of what clothes are, an illusion is created of clothing without use. In consumer culture, there's no requirement for garments to be used, only bought.

Consumerism shapes the prevailing experience of fashion

Dig a little deeper and we see other forces at play. It soon becomes apparent that the prevailing experience of fashion production and consumption is locked into a cycle of self-justification, creating the very conditions by which it becomes both dominant and credible. In consumerist fashion, the cycle of new products introduced in store becomes more rapid (up to 12 seasons per year and moving towards a strategy of continuous replenishment)[1] because retailers compete on newness. Indeed perhaps no industry has better perfected the cycle of invention, acceptance and discard of a continually changing series of temporary modes of appearance, than fashion. Nor has any sector so successfully de-linked a cycle of change from physical need or function. In the fashion context rarely does a new item better protect our bodies physically or offer enhanced functionality; rather we buy afresh to make visible our identity both as an individual and part of larger social groups, showing our currency, our 'value', through our changing dress. There is also a material component at play: we buy items more often because the downward pressure on price leads to actual or perceived deteriorating standards of material and construction – the 'quality fade'[2] – and pieces fall apart increasingly quickly and need to be replaced, necessitating another visit to the store. It seems that in contemporary consumer culture we organise our ideas about fashion around commerce and consumerism and end up becoming dependent on them.

The fashion industry itself has evolved under this narrative. The dynamics of the sector, its business models and manufacturing approaches have been reshaped by tenets of growth, globalisation and 'more and cheaper'. In the first decade of the 21st century, clothing prices in Europe fell by 26.2% and in the US by 17.1%[3] and cheap garments have also changed patterns of consumption: during that same decade the number of pieces bought in the UK increased by one third[4]; that is, to a volume of two million tonnes per annum.[5] In a merging of free market ideology, changing business practices and technological development, the sector has generated more opportunities for shoppers to consume. Prices have reduced as global tariffs on trade of textiles and clothing have relaxed and the majority of production relocated to low labour cost nations. Lead times have shortened as manufacturing of trend sensitive pieces has returned to regions of high consumption to quicken their time to market. The frequency of stock drops in store has increased as just in time manufacturing is co-ordinated with electronic sales receipts to trigger replenishment production. For fashion brands, success is measured in retail sales figures reported as a percentage growth year on year; a success that is evidenced by data which suggest that nearly 70% of garments in a wardrobe are inactive,[6] a surfeit which proves no barrier to producers in manufacturing more clothes and to consumers in buying additional new pieces.

Alternative experiences are forgotten

Within this distinctive hierarchy of fashion provision and its ideology of continuous market growth, independent and shared expectations of creating fashion have been increasingly forgotten. For instance, home sewing and mending, which used to be common relatively widely across social classes, ages and genders, has become increasingly restricted as the economic incentive to transform cloth into clothing and keep it clean and serviceable has been undercut by the cheap price of, and ready access to, new garments. Where it is still practiced, dressmaking and knitting – which experienced a revival in recent years of recession and perhaps also as a real-world reaction to a rise in virtual living and the digital economy – is often the preserve either of highly skilled 'crafter', or a badge of youthful experimentation, rather than a widespread and accepted fashion practice on a par with shopping for clothes. Further, sewing machine repair services, drapers and haberdashers are increasingly marginalised, disappearing from town centres, thereby isolating the business of maintaining and caring for garments from their purchase. While there is evidence that people often also feel unsatisfied with clothes that they have made for themselves,[7] hinting perhaps that home-production is no panacea, it seems that consumerist expectations of fashion reinforce the marginal aspect and individual idiosyncrasy of non–market fashion activity, framing them as temporary involvements to be dabbled with for a few short years before graduating to the 'proper stuff': new shop-bought clothes.

This state of affairs is not a conspiracy of the fashion industry alone, in which consumers are but forced and reluctant victims consuming more than they would otherwise do; rather it is a symptom of wider economic logic and goals, business priorities, societal forces and combined individual practices. Fashion is not bound in a fixed and narrow relationship with novelty driven consumerism as part of some sort of 'natural order'; rather its relationship answers to particular strategies and tactics. Today these tactics are by and large those of the dominant mode of capitalist production.[8] Fashion is implicated in the wider systems of control and power of the modern era. Framed like this, our majority experience of fashion becomes exposed as a way to expand the control of those with influence, as a power structure, rather than a reflection of fashion's wider potential and practice. Also uncovered is the realisation that the type of fashion experienced today is not freely chosen by citizens or shoppers: for it is often the only option.[9] Neither are the fashion alternatives freely ignored, but rather these same shoppers simply do not know about them. Instead it is the dominant ideas about economics, business practice, organisational structures, cultural preferences, and what individuals do and how they imagine their clothes, which dictate the prevailing view and experience of fashion and repress alternative ideas, stifling them, forcing them to the margins.

Yet if we choose to look to the margins, other fashion ideas and formulations are present and multifarious. In the craft of use stories clustered under the theme of 'alternative dress codes', the 'one economy' view of fashion is broken apart and is pixelated into many broader-than-market priorities. In these stories fashion provision and expression becomes a function of gifts, colour, fragile materials, memories, storytelling, pockets, knowledge, the weather, low-metal garment fasteners, age. The stories portray people confidently reimagining clothes in contexts different to those that were originally intended. They show people listening to their own internal processes and preferences and boldly inserting these into the external world.

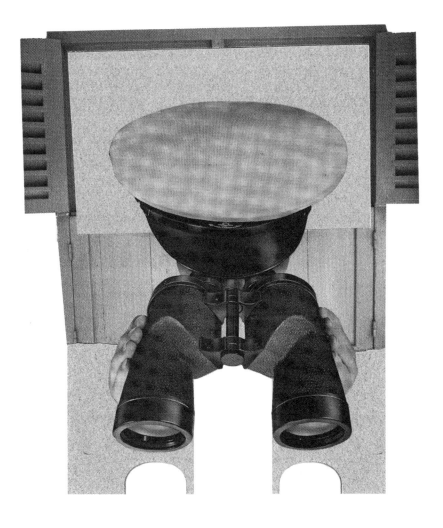

'If we choose to look to the margins ...'

The stories of 'alternative dress codes'

The choices we make about what we wear are influenced by our past experiences, our present choices and desires, and our ideas about our future selves. Expressions of values, aspirations, heritage, understanding and the physical shape of our bodies build a rationale for dress that transcends narrow commercial views about fashion. They give us broader perspectives that honour our reality as well as our aspirations; and connect our psyche with our fibre and fashion choices.

The last time

This shirt was my mother's. And it's from the 70s and I can remember her wearing it. And it's almost so fragile that it will break any minute. Because it's you know, so worn, it will fall apart ... it's almost there. Every time I wear it I wear it as if for the last time.

Kolding, Denmark, 2012

Style evolved together

Everything I'm wearing is a gift from somebody else and
that's increasingly the way my wardrobe is coming together.

  I live in New Zealand but I'm from Ireland and my mother
sends me a lot of clothes. The ladies in the administration office
will attest to that … ! It's become this dialogue between us. It
gives her a lot of joy and it also gives me a lot of joy to have this
garment that makes me think of her, that is, I'm wearing and
I'm connected to and I don't know maybe replaces that physical
touch that I can't hug her, I can't – as much as technology allows

me to connect with her – I can't be beside her … She loves shopping for me and thinking about what will bring me joy.

Sometimes she buys duplicates of the garments so she has one and I have one as well. I know it sounds really cheesy. When she came over to visit we ended up in the same garment a lot of the time. So we'd have the same coat on at the same time. We went whale watching in Kaikoura and we both had the same coat and I think there was a time when, gosh, any kind of similar appearance to my mum – like as a teenager you know you want to slightly distance yourself and create your own identity. But it's this weird maturing place I'm in where I actually quite enjoy it.

My dad was teasing us that we're like sisters now. It's kind of a nice place to be, simultaneously daughter, sister, friend. It looks different [on each of us]. We've got quite different physiques. She's about my height. I'm an inch taller – she doesn't like that. But she wouldn't be as busty as I am and I've got curly hair, she's got straight blond hair. And she's quite slim. I'm a little bit more curvy. So it does take on different characteristics.

And it's kind of funny because I think it's like our tastes have merged and it's like her style and my style have kind of evolved and come together. And sometimes she sees things in a different way. Like I may not have bought this dress for myself. But it's quite interesting, I like aspects of it … it mightn't be the version of myself that I recognise but I appreciate that she sees me in another way. I do feel [a sense of relief from not having to make a decision of what to wear] to a certain extent. I do feel a sense of guilt that I have more stuff and I probably have enough. I definitely have enough. It's a mixed feeling.

They kind of take me to somewhere I wouldn't have necessarily thought of. So like for me, I'm curious about everything and want to know as much as I can about different things so it shows me a different perspective and takes me on a different path or a different journey and I think people's appearance or their attitude to life is an evolving state so it's a reminder that I can't dictate everything, I can't plan everything and sometimes being open to different perspectives is good and can take you somewhere else.

Wellington, New Zealand, 2013

Free rein parrot fashion

There was a bet, an ill placed bet, between a friend and my
boyfriend and the loser was supposed to buy me the parrot
headband. He lost. But then my boyfriend said he didn't
want me to have it, so she bought it for me anyway.

My approach to fashion is that you should wear something
every day that makes you smile. It's hard not to smile when
you look in a mirror and see a parrot. I think if you're wearing a
parrot on your head, then you've got kind of free rein or licence
to do whatever you want.

But basically the way I approach it is that I pick one or two
things that I want to wear that day and then the rest of the
outfit comes because I try and, like, construct a story around
it and think what this imaginary person in this imaginary
situation would do. So today I really wanted to wear these
trousers ... and they're obviously very military ... so I came up
with the idea of this woman who is in the fashion militia who
has to go on this secret mission in the jungle, hence the parrot.
And then the vintage military jacket followed and my shirt
with epaulettes so it just becomes a silly little thing that I do ...

London, UK, 2012

Colour contrary

I'm wearing my usual clothing, I dress like this all the time,
no matter where I go, no matter what I do … I dress like this
for a funeral. I wear colourful clothes, always.

    I always aim to do the exact opposite of what everybody
is doing. So everybody dresses drab and dark and boring, and
I do the opposite. And I do that in just about all aspects of my
life … I realise [I am] being contrary to everybody else … in my
opinion the world is upside-down. And it should be flipped. So
I do my best. I think everybody should dress like I do (laughs).

Vancouver, Canada, 2013

Quality lessons

Well this cardigan is my mother's. She bought it when she
was around my age, in her twenties. And she's worn it ever
since ... until recently, [now she feels] it's too flashy for her
and so she said, 'you can wear it'... It's lasted for almost
thirty years ... the sense of buying good quality stuff is
natural to her ... It makes me realise, she has been teaching
me that all this time ...

Vancouver, Canada, 2013

Six pockets

This is a very prosaic Gore-Tex rain jacket. It's like my number
one favourite garment. For two reasons. One, it's the ideal
piece of outerwear for San Francisco. You know, because the
weather changes often … good for a windbreaker, it's totally
versatile. And the other thing I like about it, is it has eight
pockets. So it's totally good for logistics because I'm a logistics
person. I love garments with pockets … A utility belt, that's
what you need. Or a fisherman's vest, I'd love to have one
of those, except you look so dorky!

I have to have a minimum of six [pockets in every garment].
That's just because I wear glasses so I need a place to put the
case, a place to put the phone – it doesn't put the same place
as the case because the phone will get scratched. And then
you know I have other bad habits which require their own
pocket. And I have a pencil and notepad in one pocket and
wallet and keys in one so you know you fill up your six pockets
pretty quick.

San Francisco, USA, 2012

Stay warm

The way I use clothes is I stay warm. There's the jacket and
the hat and the cowl and the scarf. And this sable thing gets
tied and goes ass first, head in the back. The sables go on when
it gets below 40. Everything else, yeah I guess you could say
that it gets layered with ... cold ... it has been obscenely cold.

New York City, USA, 2013

Dress to honour all parts of my life

My god daughter lived in India so I got the material for the
red dress in India and then I had it made up by a Sardinian
dressmaker back here [in the UK] … It's red because
I'm a socialist. I wear red a lot. But I'm also wearing my
grandmother's engagement ring, earrings made for me by my
brother-in-law, ring made by my sister-in-law and a necklace
given to me by my husband. And because I've got nothing
from my mother because she died when I was young I've got
tights with seams up the back because that's all I can remember
about my mother was that she used to have seamed stockings.

London, UK, 2011

Ready made identity

I kind of think of my shirt as, like, dressing to fulfil as
many roles in the society as possible with the least amount
of energy and the least amount of capital expenditure and the
most amount of up-cycling. If I could I s'pose I'd go to thrift
stores like I used to 'cos that's a pleasurable, kind of, prolonged
experience of sorting through smells and textures and stuff
and it's usually better stuff than you can buy new.

   So what do I do? I go to a place called Lands End Inlet.
It's not an outlet. It's called an inlet and what they do there;
it's a place full of returns and this is the most convenient
place in my remote part of New York State. I shop [there]
because they have a seemingly endless supply of shirts in
my precise size but are monogrammed with different people's
names who didn't like [them]. So I buy these monogrammed
shirts and I either pull out the stitching if I have time or I
wear them with the sleeves rolled up so no-one knows that I'm
not JMC or ODM or whatever else it is. It's kind of funny, you
know, my students they look at me like I'm a conservative guy
or something or dressing for some bureaucratic function but
I guess we need to choose one of these identities – off the peg
identities – right? Off the garment rack. Ready-made identities.
They're doing the same thing really but they think they're
expressing their individuality and I have no misconceptions
that I'm neither looking too smart nor looking too creative.

San Francisco, USA, 2011

Low metal

I go into prisons and teach basic computing skills. However, I learned quickly that you have to create sort of a personality [through your dress] that's authoritative … It was also important when I was putting different ensembles together, that I try to be as low metal as possible, or if the metal exists, pure metal, because it makes a lot less cumbersome when I am going through the metal detectors. Sometimes very fine pieces of clothing that had tiny little clasps set them off, and I've had things like large earrings or the ring that I have, that never go off at all … so [in a process of elimination] I just go through one day and find out what works and what doesn't and start paring down.

New York City, USA, 2013

Strategy for old age

This clothing decision is a strategy for dealing with old age.
One of the things that happens when you get older is your
feet actually get long 'cos your arch drops and so the shoes I've
been wearing for years which I adore were suddenly too small.
And so the problem became what to buy that I could wear that
would be entirely comfortable so they're these, alright? They
do look like you're a Ninja turtle because they're very like,
clumpy and foolish which my wife pointed out almost
immediately. They have a magical foam in the sole that during
the first ten hours of wear forms itself to your foot only so
they are my own shoes and when I bought them I knew that
these were the shoes but for some reason the company went
out of business so I immediately went to eBay and bought
what I consider to be a lifetime's supply – 4 pairs!

San Francisco, USA, 2011

Style by heritage

This is a sport coat that my father wore all through my youth.
The coat was reminiscent of my father's casual, entertaining
times and I like to, sort of, live on the tradition so even if it's
not exactly the most appropriate thing to wear I will sport it
and it seems to do alright. I wouldn't say it's my particular style
by like what I define myself by but it's definitely my style by
heritage, I guess. Like regardless of what I want my style to
be like, this is my style, sort of, permanently. I have a picture
of my dad and his brother [in my wallet] in suits when they
were like three or four years old. They grew up in a very formal
household in Chicago and he was born in 1929 wearing suits
everyday as children.

San Francisco, USA, 2011

Use: a disruptive technology

The presence of other types of fashion expression that record examples of fashion outside of the logic of growth work to change the luminosity and significance of the context of use. They begin to loosen the binds that keep use practices below ground. They reflect (audaciously?) the reality of the situation: clothes are used! The stories show that despite contributing little or nothing to fashion industry trade or growth; despite not being seen as valuable activity by measures like GDP; despite the associated skills and competencies having no currency in fashion circles; we tend and wear our garments over and again. In the face of forces that scream the opposite, people are acting in ways that are resourceful and motivated by a deep knowledge and satisfaction with what they have. Practices of use exist beyond the market.

The stories also tell that, notwithstanding the priorities of the market economy, beyond-the-market activity is an essential part of the fashion system. They frame design and use as part of the same whole: design is empty without use; use impossible without design. The one changes the other. In adding the life-world of users of clothes to the dynamics of fashion-as-industry, we grow fashion beyond design and production. For some it is an uncomfortable prospect, as when ideas about the priorities of fashion business extend to include those who wear a piece tomorrow and in a decade's time, taking up a hem and pinning a pocket along the way, power geometries alter. Control shifts as the multiple contingencies of a web of future lives and ongoing time are factored in. There is jeopardy here. Paying attention to use assumes that fashion will be shaped from bedroom floors and wardrobes as much as from boardrooms and design studios. It also assumes that we conceive of a way to create fashion jointly as an enterprise between supply chains and users, between the demands of today and the more distant, but no less urgent, needs of the future (see Chapter 6). The context and practices of use are a disruptive technology for fashion, they interrupt existing market priorities and value networks. They are charged with different patterns of power, with citizen politics that spans wider than government, with practical wisdom gleaned from our own, individual, subjective, surprising lives.

If this sounds like revolution, then perhaps it is. Though it is a revolution in which we are already participating often quietly and through small acts, including the ongoing use of clothing – as evidenced by the nearly 500 people interviewed as part of the *Local Wisdom* project. It seems that a focus on the practices of use recasts garments as objects of optimism, vessels of hope for the future – like in the craft of use stories of 'mixed use' below – and gives us pause to wonder what might happen if we feted users as we do creators and explicitly celebrated ongoing tending and wear?

In design work that accompanied the recording of stories of the craft of use, some of these questions were tentatively explored. The project *A Love Story*, by a group of designers from the Kolding School of Design in Denmark, took as its starting point the idea that garments and the people who wear them are not islands apart from production – or each other. Here a radical garment is one that maps these relationships and brings them out of the shadows; that explores what is around and between us. The *Love Story* garments have been designed as a pair using magnetism. Tiny magnets and metal beads are sewn into the garment's fabric to seek to connect and relate it to the wider world. These conceptual pieces are the beginning of an idea that counters and develops our usual experience of fashion, upending a view of fashion as isolated objects creating instead something that becomes a valuable fashion expression through its associations with others.

A Love Story by Marie Munk Hartwig, Nina Lolle and Signe Skovgaard Klok

The stories of 'mixed use'

Irrespective of design intention, a garment can sometimes
meet many needs, functioning in ways that are unplanned
and idiosyncratic. Such a piece calls into being a way
of thinking that is primed for finding more diverse
potential in fashion garments and opens a door to
increased possibilities of use.

Two-piece apron

So, I have this amazing two-piece garment that I found at
a thrift store. It was in dead-stock condition and it had no
labels on it. So I had no idea what time period it came from
or where it was from. But I really appreciated the construction
of it ... both pieces are worn like an apron so you can wear
them over other pieces ... together or separately ... [one piece]
has this big hood on it. They're this heavy [fabric], a brushed
cotton twill ... it's all about the ... the durability of it and
its versatility ...

New York City, USA, 2013

Coat sled

This is my fur coat. It's beaver. It is from Alaska and is very
heavy. It takes everything [to make it] and it's not nice in
that way. But it is absolutely warm. It was my mother who
bought it. It had been on sale because there had been a fire
in the shop and they had to get rid of everything. So my
mother went there and she came home with three fur coats.

And I got the biggest one. It was okay, just a bit curly in
the middle from the fire but nothing more. It was thick
and big and gleaming.

Our [Norwegian national] hero Nansen used fur under
his skis when he went out in the ice [during Polar expeditions]
because it goes very fast when [the nap] is down, and then
it sticks to ice [when against the run of the nap] and keeps
you going up.

And I used the fur coat in the same way. I would sit my
children on my stomach and then we just Shwoooosht!!!
I had to go head first to get the fur the right way. And they
were very happy for that, you know? And I really almost
had a massage of my back … I used it very often. At last
it was my children's children who sat on my stomach.
So it's very old you know.

And then it comes to this where you can't use a fur
coat anymore [as it is morally and socially unacceptable].
So then I packed the beaver down in newspaper, down
in a trunk where it was for many years. But in 2010 we
got the really cold weather in Norway and my jacket wasn't
warm enough and then I gradually took out the newspaper.
And it hadn't changed … Surely when you have these
old things it's better to wear something now that it's
been made rather than throw it away?

Oslo, Norway, 2012

Year-round coat

This is an old Burberry coat of my mother's – Sandra – from the 80s. They don't make this kind anymore. It's super long. It's like this cotton-twill but it somehow really repels water … and it has zip-in-zip-out lining which is the key part because I live in New York and so we are outside all the time and it requires lots of thought about how to equip yourself at any given moment. It's kind of a year-round coat. When I first moved back to New York I didn't have a whole lot of money or a job so my mum gave me this coat and then since then my mum actually tried to replace this coat with a newer version and it has fallen apart because I don't think it's made in the same way or in the same place or with the same fabric.

San Francisco, USA, 2011

Fostering change: ground …

Sustainability presents innumerable challenges for fashion, many of which are deeply rooted in the foundational structures of the sector; structures in need of overhauling. As we face them and embrace the potential of use, I find great encouragement in American poet Gary Snyder's counsel about knowing and living fully in our situation. He suggests we do two things.[10]

The first: locate and ground ourselves in our actual condition. For Snyder this means, 'know[ing] north from south, pine from fir, in which direction the new moon might be found, where the water comes from, where the garbage goes, how to shake hands, how to sharpen a knife, how the interest rates work'. In the fashion context, this grounding means knowing the deep-rooted political and structural influence of the market and individualistic consumption on our ideas about fashion in order to better understand its influence on us. It means we recognise contemporary fashion culture's superficiality and impermanence and our imaginative dependency on it. It also means we acknowledge that fashion is often positioned as the epitome of value-free expression, equipping us to appear in a world that is not rooted in the vitality of earth, the health of its soil or its people; but rather one that is 'essentially groundless' and a 'world of ideas'.[11] In this imaginary, emotional and physic world almost anything is possible – fashion is light and free – there are few limits. This is part of fashion's power and appeal. Yet it has been appropriated by the market and in its commodification, in its transformation of idea to physical garment, fashion comes up against serious limits.

Planetary boundaries restrict and demarcate all human activity, including the production of fibre, fabric and garment. Agricultural land is finite and that turned over to growing fibre for textiles cannot be used for the cultivation of other, perhaps more essential, crops like food. Access to clean water is becoming increasingly contested as populations rise, pollution increases and we divert more of it to dye fabric and launder clothes in our homes. Thus to read fashion as free-floating and limitless is to see fashion out of context with the physical and ecological systems that give it material form. This creates an anachronistic form of fashion. Fashion, by definition, reflects its context; a context that patently includes its people, its ecosystems, its soil. So when we frame fashion as 'limitless' and/or achievable only through ever-greater consumption; it seems this blinkered 'performance' is quite simply, no longer fashion.

… and stray

After first grounding ourselves, the second thing to do, says Snyder, is to stray outside:

> One departs the home to embark on a quest into an archetypal wilderness that is dangerous, threatening, and full of beasts and hostile aliens. This sort of encounter with the other – both the inner and the outer – requires giving up comfort and safety, accepting cold and hunger, and being willing to eat anything. You may never see home again. Loneliness is your bread. Your bones may turn up someday in some riverbank mud. It grants you freedom, expansion, and release. Untied. Unstuck. Crazy for a while. It breaks taboos, it verges on transgression, it teaches humility.[12]

To stray is to roam free from the understanding and epistemologies associated with the 'current condition'. To act differently, to think afresh, to update our ideas about what it is to know about fashion and sustainability in order to re-appreciate the potential of fashion to nourish and foster other actions. As we 'stray' for sustainability's sake from the dominant narrative or 'project of realization'[13] that prevails in fashion today, we uncover new perspectives in which to locate sustainability opportunities that change both *what* we consume, impacting levels of resource consumption, and *how* we consume, altering our practices and ideas and ultimately our relationship with clothing over the long term.

In paying attention to the context and practices of use, we transgress outside growth–logic and establish a fashion presence outside of a market-driven cycle of consumer desire and demand. The craft of use sees alternatives nourished and reared in open acknowledgement of – not subjugation to – conventional expectations of fashion;

'The skills of the craft of use'

broadening the fashion conversation, extending the types of fashion expression found valuable. By highlighting other fashion experiences we see ourselves in a broader relational web than fashion-as-shopping. We begin to link garments and our actions to ideas bigger than ourselves, a lively part in a livelier whole. We may forge associations where before we may have sensed none, creating and strengthening resilience between and within individual and systems. And in so doing, we take a small step to weaken the isolated, autonomous, socially indifferent view of fashion that typifies consumerist fashion priorities.

The stories of 'skills of resourcefulness' reveal some of these directions of travel and show ways we can begin to love the space between fashion and the world. They reveal how individual agency, and lives of the people who wear clothes, can add to the flows of economic capital of the formal sector. They also raise many questions. Including what do the fashion-related actions and skills of the public reveal about the alternatives to consumerism within the sector? What do they tell us about the ways in which we can add data about people's actions, choices and behaviour, including about use, to established types of fashion knowledge so as to better attune the fashion system to the bigger systems?

The stories of 'skills of resourcefulness'

Creative activists contribute greatly to society through
innovation and experiment, taking on projects that fail
to hit the radar of conventional industry. Their work
is a training ground for new practices, for trialling
novel approaches and reviving old skills that promote
alternative ideas about fashion provision and consumption.

Special things come second-hand

What I am wearing today is nothing new and possibly a family
affair, the skirt that I am wearing was once a 'house coat' –
it was in my mom's wardrobe for a long time, and I thought
it was so glamorous, but when I put it on I did feel like I was
wearing a dressing gown so I've done a very crude chopping off
of the top. I am not a great sewer so ... pins, and buttons, but it's
a beautiful cotton. Yes, it's lost the button, it's lost a few things.

And this is a fantastic spotted silk top that I found in a local
vintage store and I don't know why but I was very impressed
that it was made in Italy (laughs). It's just that European style
that us Australian's crave. It might be a pre-conceived notion
of how things are made now, but I love the idea that things
were possibly made on a smaller scale and with more care, and
better quality, from a time when people really loved and wore
and used their clothes in a different way.

I just can't get over how much pleasure I get from second
hand clothes ... They give a lot of happiness ... My first
experience of what I thought was glamour was going to the
Inglewood op shop, in the little town near where I grew up.

We would buy negligees, they were full-length dresses on my
sister and I as little girls. And we would be running round the
farm in gumboots and negligees tied in knots. So for me, special
things really came from second-hand shops from a young age.

Melbourne, Australia, 2013

Teddy bear accessory

I brought my genuine teddy bear fur coat. I traded in a pair
of Doc Martens for this coat and I haven't even felt the cold …
I always buy things second hand but I trade when I can.
Sometimes they don't want what I got (laughs). And I also
like things that don't require me to bring a lot of accessories …
I like how this already has a hood to it … I don't have to bring
a hat. I always lose those.

New York City, USA, 2013

Piece and pattern

My step grandmother that I never met passed away …
they were getting rid of all of her clothes … and there
was this giant Mumu [dress] in her closet. The edges
aren't finished, it is not serged [overlocked] or anything.
So it turned out that she'd made it because I later found
the pattern for it, and took that as well. I will make more
of these dresses.

Vancouver, Canada, 2013

Skills trialled in Kleenex

These are things that my mother made for herself that she
passed on to me. I have this skirt, it's tweed I think and it
has a matching coat. And I don't know, I don't really remember
her wearing it but I like to wear it together. Because it is
so unexpected now! There is also this vest, that's reversible.
So the inside is made from an old mole fur coat that belonged
to my grandmother and then it started getting a bit thread
bare, so my mom cut it apart and made it into this reversible
vest. And this sort of woven fabric, I don't know where
she got it, she was always just buying things. They had to
be cheap. She never wanted to spend any money and at some
point she decided that fabrics stores were just too expensive
and so instead buying at thrift stores and re-fashioning.
    My mom taught herself to sew. She said that she taught herself
by making clothes with Kleenex [paper handkerchiefs] for her
dolls when she was a little, like really small. And then she started
sewing. She tried to teach me but she was so good at it that
she couldn't break it down enough to show me … When I was
14 I took a course … but I broke every sewing machine …

Vancouver, Canada, 2013

Skilling up

This top is made from the first pattern that I ever cut
and it's made from an old tablecloth that I found in a charity
shop. It's a new step for me … doing my own thing with it.

Dublin, Ireland, 2012

Thrift treasure

This is a wool jacket I bought it at a thrift store with my
grandmother in Oregon in 2007 and the label is Gianni Petite,
made in the USA … It's a really lovely wool. It's fine and soft
and very warm and absolutely ideal for San Francisco. It's not
too heavy, not too thick. It's a great weight. I like the fact it's
made in the USA.

   You can't really find that anymore, especially something
of this quality and the fact I found it with my grandmother is
also special for me … I grew up thrifting with her. She's very
frugal. She grew up during the Depression and she only buys
stuff in thrift stores. Everything in her home; her furniture,
her cookware, her clothes, everything is from thrift stores.
And I've definitely learned how to thrift because of her …
to recognise good fabric … It can't be a blend. She only does
100%. So I'm able now to go down the aisles really quickly
and sometimes just through touching or sometimes just visually
finding the pieces of clothing that stand out due to the material
they're made out of. I've had women offer me hundreds of
dollars for this jacket on the street and it's amazing how many
women ask me, 'where did you get that? I love that coat'.

San Francisco, USA, 2011

Investment of time

When I saw this sweater in the shop I could see it had value because of the time spent making it [it is hand knitted] but since it had mother of pearl buttons, I didn't know how to use it because it didn't have that style that I really liked … but after some years I changed the buttons I knew suddenly how to mix it with different things, how to use it and now I am really happy about it.

Kolding, Denmark, 2012

Thrifting since '77

Everything I have on is from thrift stores. I have gotten things
that I own, the majority of clothing items and jewellery items
that I own since 1977 in thrift shops. I do not buy first-hand
items. Dress from a thrift store. Shoes from a thrift store,
stockings from a thrift store, under garments. You name it.
I can also always see a garment that is my size and my styles
– variety of styles – the minute I go into a shop. I'm part Italian
… and I always can spy the Italian outfit in even a huge thrift
shop … Will walk in the door and I will almost instantly see
the outfit that will fit me and is made in Italy. I just see them.
I've gotten to the point where they just jump out at me.

San Francisco, USA, 2011

3

Matter in Motion

The Stories of Open and Adjust,
Garment Co-operation
and Easy Repair

In his superlative 1967 account of a winter of watching and following
peregrine falcons around the Kent coast in South-Eastern England,
J. A. Baker opens with a description of contrasts between a picture
of the falcon and experience of the living bird:

> Books about birds show pictures of the peregrine … Large
> and isolated in the gleaming whiteness of the page, the hawk
> stares back at you, bold, statuesque, brightly coloured. But when
> you have shut the book, you will never see that bird again …
> The living bird will never be so large, so shiny-bright. It will be
> deep in landscape, and always sinking further back … Pictures
> are waxworks beside the passionate mobility of the living bird.[1]

In its teasing apart of the distinctions between static knowledge
and dynamic understanding, between indirect and direct experience,
this wonderful book also seems to me to shed bright light on our
understanding of fashion and its use. It perhaps reveals too, in a
small way, how fashion and birds are alike.

Like Baker's picture of the peregrine, fashion images are often poised,
striking, confident. Also like a close-up bird illustration, they reveal
almost nothing of the real-life, in-context experience of the piece
itself. Fashion is created and presented in ways that do not refer to,
or imagine, use over time. Commercial fashion imagery is directed
to the fashion offer of this one isolated moment. The images show
pieces available to *buy now*; they are unworn, uncrumpled, capturing
the idealised moment before a person slips on a piece, before time
and life enters the sleeves, marks the collar and creases the fabric at the
front hip of the trouser leg. This image becomes the reference point for
fashion. The picture – and its young, mesomorphic models and hyper-
real shoot location – offers a glimpse of clothes as part of an imaginary
world, an invented possible version of our future selves, an idea of

someone we think we might like to become. With it come fraught concerns about body image, social status, psychological security, resource consumption, conflation of identity and self-worth with clothes as a cure to life's 'problems'. These concerns are added to when, in the course of one, posed moment, an image suggests that it is possible to glean most of what is important about fashion by seeing it as a garment detached from its context of use: separate from the lives who will tend and use it, isolated from the relationships and interactions that shape whole dynamics of the broader world. The magazine shoots, the unsmiling, oddly back–tilted walk of models on a runway, the rails of as yet unworn clothes in a high street store, reveal fashion as a waxwork. It is a still life beside the varied, unpredictable, fervent, 'deep in landscape' experience that unfolds while these clothes are worn.

Thus lifted out of time and its context of use, fashion becomes an object, a vehicle for trade, a sketch on a computer screen, a digit on a spreadsheet, for which it is easy to see ourselves as separate and from which we release ourselves of responsibility. Jeremy Till describes it this way: 'When time is ignored … the object becomes a commodity of capital exchange rather than a crucible of social exchange'.[2] As a commodity apart from the context of its use, the object loses its vital, ethical associations: with people, their unfolding lives, the diverse, long term health of our communities, the soil beneath our feet. It and we both become understood as somehow 'separate, autonomous, individualistic, skin-bound, ego-bound subjects',[3] alienated from the effects of our actions, disassociated from the broader world.

But attend to the context of use of fashion, share the time of others, and we affect a shift. For this is the time and space in the lifecycle of a garment in which connections are made: life happens here. And thus we begin, in a small way, to take responsibility. We link the creation of fashion to the things that go on when the garment gets home. We see these expanding future actions and relationships as part of a shared fashion experience. We sketch the on-going activities of use of garments alongside the design of those garments – activities that help foster skills and competence. We design to build awareness about what's going on and foster ideas and confidence about what we must do. We tell stories and make images of fashion that show it as a process that works with context, with assisting, connecting to, others.

'Fashion is dependent on its surroundings for its wholeness'

Matter in motion

During the course of writing this book, I lived on the side of a hill (a 'fell') bordering a forest in the North of England. There were birds everywhere. The sky was continuously moving, flecked with darting flurries of feather and beak. I studied books to help me identify the birds, but these quickly fell out of use. They didn't help much. They rarely showed birds in flight or in mixed groups, or in habitats from the angles and views that I witnessed each day. Quite simply the books didn't capture my experience of birds. There was nothing in those pages about the rush of air on my cheek as a swallow swoops past hungry for the midges circling my head, or how flocks of goldcrest move like flutters of butterflies high in the forest canopy, or about the similarity between white-edged tails of skylark and chaffinch twisting and turning as the car flushes them out of the verges. Neither do they say much about the stillness of kestrels hunting for voles along the field edges laced with dry stone walls, or even about the plaintive cry of the curlew on the moors, so melancholic and resonant that it presses on your heart. I did eventually learn the birds' names but only after I learnt their haunts and ways of moving, their calls, their markings, their funny habits and how they made me feel. Ornithology, like fashion, is enriched by direct experience. Neither birds nor clothes are static objects, totalised by a drawing on a page, our experience of both of them is far greater than their image, but rather (after Lucretius), they are *matter in motion*. We know them differently because of their liveliness and the endless variation of the context in which we experience them. Bird and fashion both is dependent on its surroundings for its wholeness.

Some of the most convincing insights to emerge about fashion in a post-growth scenario from the craft of use stories are rooted in this dynamic, subjective, direct experience of the world. They reveal fashion as an open-ended process, made fuller by being adaptable and responsive to the unpredictable phenomena that occur in everyday life. They show that fashion has within it types of knowledge that stretch out in four dimensions: across the three dimensions of cloth and body in space plus the dimension of time. Moreover, these stories encapsulate processes of change that take place not just to garments as they are worn, but also to us, their users, as we wear them, as we grow, laugh, learn in and because of them. This is perhaps testament to what philosopher Jane Bennett calls vital materialism,[4] a life and agency present in the non-human world that shapes the human one. This élan vital enriches our discernment of the force of things, underlining our sense that everything is connected and our feelings of satisfaction dependent on them.

The group of craft of use stories clustered under the title of 'open and adjust' are full of this lively matter, thanks at least in part to them being such happy, blatant expressions of agency and creativity. They showcase some of the material manipulations already done with clothes by users past the point of purchase, they constitute hands-on reworking of pieces and all of the subtleties, and roughness, involved therein. Their material starting points are wildly different – nothing is off limits: any type of fibre will do; any fabric construction; any size. Woven cloth is augmented with knitted panels; garments designed to be worn one way around are turned the other; buttons added, reflective strips added, sequins added. Cloth cut away, cloth sewn in. On the way, already proficient makers practise their skills, and less proficient ones, learn them. Not only that but ideas about other ways with garments are born and questions posed about revising established ways of doing things: why can't you buy half a yard of the same fabric your dress is made from, so you can alter it?

The stories of 'open and adjust'

Garments can be reworked to meet changing needs.
The knowledge and skills to open up a garment and
adjust it to fit contribute to a rich and confident society.
They remind us about ingenuity and resourceful possibility
and help replace consumption with action.

Cycling wonder

I am wearing a reconstructed Nicola Finetti dress. It's a
seventies silk wonder. So I've remade it so the sleeves are
the legs and it's designed for cycling, so there are attachable
pockets that detach. I have reflective elements, for visibility,
and as you are riding these sort of flap in the wind and expose
the hi vis elements ... It's now a jumpsuit. It's a onesie.

Melbourne, Australia, 2013

Button vertebrae

This is a very old cashmere cardigan which has quite a strong connection with my mum. She's quite a hoarder and I've inherited that off her. And I have a habit, whenever I go home, of sort of going through her things and then persuading her that she doesn't wear them anymore and that they should be passed on to me.

So this is one of those that I think she must have got from a jumble sale or a charity shop. I've customised it by sewing on these buttons. I found that when I wore it, I actually liked to wear it back to front with the buttons done up the back. But to make it look more purposeful I decided to sew on all these little shell buttons here which are from a sort of collection of buttons that again my mum had – I think as she's worn through cardigans she tends to snip the buttons off and end up felting up the cardigan. So these are from old cardigans. And I quite like the way that if you wear it the right way round you end up with buttons sort of running down your spine like vertebrae. But then if you wear it that way round, it's sort of in the place of where the buttons would go.

London, UK, 2012

Three stage jacket

I call this my three stage jacket. It began about forty years
ago as a very slim waistcoat that was given to me. So I put
a [knitted] panel into the back just to be able to fasten it
together at the front, you see. And then about fifteen years
ago I started going to sessions of an international folk dancing
group in Chorlton, near Manchester. So in order to have a
jacket appropriate for the Balkans, I added sleeves, a collar
and some trimmings. And then, only about five years ago,
I became a bit too big to button it up so I added latchets
across to it, you see, and that's how it is at the moment.

Bollington, UK, 2009

Tear off the bottom, paint over the logo

My jacket … I just tore off the bottom cause it's a normal
trench coat and I would feel a bit too stiff or too fancy
if I wear it all the way down … I rarely buy new clothes.
I don't like logos, generally and remove them if it wouldn't
ruin the clothes … I just don't want to go flash around that
I wear brands and I don't want people to think that I have
some agenda … be categorised as some type, or something …

Kolding, Denmark, 2012

Half a yard

I bought the dress to match the shoes. The shoes are adorable
and I had to have the perfect dress. And I found it but it
was a halter neck with a back out. This was for an evening
function for church and I thought I don't want my total back
out, so … I bought two [identical] dresses and used the front
of one dress to make the back of this one to close in the halter
… The buttons that were on the other dress I added to the
front. I had a little shoulder wrap too in this fabric and the
rest I used to make a little bag …

You get something in the store and it's not quite right, it
would be nice if a separate piece of fabric came with it, you
know just enough, so that if you wanted to do something
different with it … You could do a lot with a yard or even half
a yard, if you just wanted to cover up some cleavage or add the
hem; half a yard even would do, even at an extra cost. It's just
that you can't match it when you go to a fabric shop usually.
And this dress was $167, and I bought two because I was so
adamant about having the correct colour …

Marin City, USA, 2012

Inside-out

This jacket I'm wearing now, my mother also wore it. She's
the one that sewed it from another jacket which was originally
my father's, a long big suede jacket, down to the knees. He
bought his in 1962 in a small town in Sweden. In 1964 he
had an accident driving his scooter and [the jacket] was ripped.
My mother thought the leather was still beautiful ... She took
it apart and she discovered the smooth leather on the inside ...
so then she turned it [inside-out]. And so all that she needed
to make this jacket then was some [cuff] braid. And this button
which was an original as well and also this bit ... And what
is funny is that this style ... is 1970s, that's when she actually
took this leather and made something out of it. So a 1970s
style which originated from a 1960s jacket.

Oslo, Norway, 2012

Skills learnt online

I'm wearing a dress that's made with an extra large T-shirt
[sewn together with] the bottom of an actual dress I had at
home saved. It didn't fit me well … It was very large. I tried
making it smaller on the top but it didn't work out so I just
cut the bottom off and attached it to the T-shirt … [I learned
to sew] by myself by looking online and experimenting.

San Francisco, USA, 2012

Sweater age 4

I love failed handicrafts ... semi-finished ... I have a collection
of clothing I have made [from such things]. I like both to make
them and to think of the first maker and why she gave up ...
and about what I would have said to help her further. I think
of the knowledge that is needed to use simple techniques to
achieve beautiful things ...

This top was a small sweater size about 4 years ... I [picked
it up as I] make quilts from old knitted garments ... But it was
so cute! So I tried to keep some of the 'cute' and make it large
enough for my body. I used the arms and [shaped them into]
the side and shoulder. In addition [I added some] crochet so
there was some air – and also [to make it] slightly larger.

Most of my clothes are made or given or found. I've never
bought clothes for myself ... with some very few exceptions ...
As a child my mum made clothes. And so I began quite small ...

Oslo, Norway, 2012

A skein of relationships changing over time

Examples of garment reworking and adaption, like those above, signal strongly that in the lives and minds of users of clothes, fashion provision and expression are fluid and changeable. They gesture that fashion is as much process, practice and performance as garment. And that to use clothes is to engage with a course of evolution and editing, wearing, waiting and taking action in co-ordination with the pieces themselves.

'A new relationship dependent not on what fashion is, but what it enables'

Here, clothing is continuously seen as ripe and ready for change, with few fixed start or finish points, occurring as flows of fibre, fabric and thread in the process of – in the way of – use. The cloth and we, the users, are part of a process of transformation. It is a route to an experience characterised not by what we have, but by an authentic sense of being in the world, 'a mastering of one's person'.[5] A new relationship with fashion is uncovered in such moments of fashion provision and expression: dependent not on what fashion is, but what it enables; not a 'need for' something, but a 'need to do' something.[6]

Put differently, it is a shift in focus from fashion as material object to a fashion-ability, an ability founded in the relationship between person and piece. This brings to mind Lao Tzu's wonderful *Tao Te Ching*[7] and the relational, sometimes counterintuitive truths of his poem, *The Uses of Not*:

> Thirty spokes
> meet in the hub.
> Where the wheel isn't
> is where it's useful.
>
> Hollowed out,
> clay makes a pot.
> Where the pot's not
> is where it is useful.
>
> Cut doors and windows
> to make a room.
> Where the room isn't,
> there's room for you.
>
> So the profit in what is
> is in the use of what isn't.

Seen through such a lens, the materiality of the wheel, the pot, the room – the garment – is revealed as part, but not all, of a larger, emergent, more–than-material process: a subsystem within a bigger whole. This active and connected conception of the world, of nested

inter-related systems, and constant interchange between them
– in which a product, its supply chain and its profit potential is
not the overarching, shaping supra-system – is, to put it mildly,
a different view from the norm.

The craft of use: a different view from the norm

Fashion, like many other sectors, has sought to quantify, predict and
control its product and supply chain, for this has allowed it to show
positive returns on the bottom line. It has pursued efficiencies at scale,
increased volumes and produced, by some measures, comfortable,
convenient pieces that 'disburden' their users of involvement with
them (also see Chapter 4). It has done this, successfully one could
argue, by cutting itself off from the context of use and all use's
attendant dependencies and uncertainty. After all, the sector's logic
goes, its goal is to engineer and facilitate the creation and sales of
clothing, not wear the things! The machine model of fashion industry
production has little place for temporal and human complexity linked
to use, no place for the multifarious activity that spins off in seemingly
every direction after the point of purchase. The act of adding knitted
back panels, then sleeves, collar, waistband and finally 'latchets' to a
simple woven waistcoat over a period of 40 years goes unheeded. It
is endearing, resourceful, time-based and wholly incongruous within
the dominant fashion story (see the tale of *Three stage jacket* p. 108).

The commercial fashion sector seeks total influence in part of a
garment's life. It cedes all control in other parts: after the point of
purchase. The imperative of sustainability requires these parts be
brought together, to better the whole, to make it more intricate,
resilient, richer, more reflective of how we live. It is a process that
requires some bold adjustment. Stewart Brand, writing about the
built environment explains it thus: 'The transition … is a leap from
the certainties of controllable things in space to the self-organising
complexities of an endlessly ravelling and unravelling skein of
relationships over time'.[8] It means, quite simply, that to *design for
sustainability* is to develop techniques and methods that allow us to
reach forwards through time and embrace the unpredictable, unformed,
ambiguous 'life world' of people and clothing. We need to empathise,

to talk to people, to develop the skills of anticipation, of rigorous imagination, of noticing, of storytelling, of prototyping new types of behaviour and the garments that encourage them.

Without such methods and skills we will fail to honour the fact that, to paraphrase Brand further, in the hands of users, garments have lives of their own.[9] And moreover, without them we neglect to recognise that these garments' lives add immeasurably to fashion. The task ahead is to bring fashion design and production together with its products' plural lives spreading forward through time. Such an opportunity changes fashion's modus operandi. It introduces a different, broader, context- and surroundings–dependent ethical frame to direct a sector in need of change; a new opportunity to, as perfectly phrased by Evans, 'improve the human condition' over its current preoccupation to display and 'express the human condition'.[10]

Yet such work is challenging. Experiences from the design projects that formed part of the *Local Wisdom* research provide a foretaste of the range of difficulties in linking traditional design practice and education to the real world and its unpredictable social data. Some projects struggled because the skills needed to design systems of garment use, including the dynamic interaction between clothing and people, aren't part of traditional fashion design training and education. In a bid to produce graduates that can hit the ground running in the current business model, education has become attuned to teaching designers to create visions for fashion objects for sale, but not for fashion objects in use. Designers are schooled in starting a creative process from visual references on a mood board but strain to supplement that with life stories and techniques and habits of use. By contrast, other designers were comfortable with stories as starting points, but expended a great deal of time and effort in gathering new tales extra to that which we already had, revealing perhaps the considerable weight given in design practice to generating unique ideas *ex nihilo* rather than building on and collaborating with what already exists. Other projects still raised concerns about ownership of ideas, about creative contribution and what role design can play when it is concerned with facilitating relations and interactions across time with things that others designed (often long ago) rather than giving form to new material products.

Designing with unknown futures

Handling ideas and practices of use of fashion over time raises a slew of questions for all involved. For designers, perhaps chief among them is how to design with unknown futures? How do we take account of the influence of a garment's context on a piece's life? How do we make the space for life and lived experience to play out in the garments of which we conceive? How do we acknowledge the contribution of others? The answers to these questions are still to be worked out – perhaps you, *Dear Reader*, can experiment? As part of the body of design research that accompanied the gathering of stories upon which this book is based, some tentative starting points have been offered up. In *Cut, Pleat, Shorten, Fit*, Anja Crabb started from the premise that most garments today are designed as 'closed', unchallengeable pieces that don't invite manipulation, or change. They don't call for alteration or unpicking but instead bear the air of shop finish and finality.

Cut, Pleat, Shorten, Fit by Anja Crabb

But what if universal garment staples – the seam, the dart, the hem – signal instead 'adjust to fit here'? Does it set a more open tone of conversation between user and clothing? In her work, a skirt and top are printed with colour-coded guidelines that mark out traditional areas of adjustment for a wide range of body shapes. Drawing on historical research from the dress archive at London College of Fashion and multiple hand–made and altered garments, these pieces promote the unique characteristics of an individual's body and life. They quietly invite us, the user, to make this garment ours.

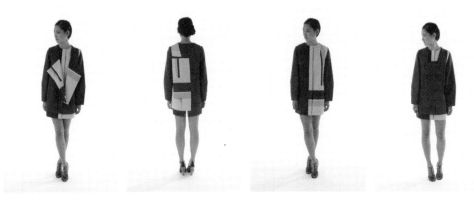

Daymaker Jacket by Lina Funder-Nielsen, Nanna Vinter Fjord and Signe Eistorp Nielsen

In another piece of design research, *Daymaker Jacket*, by a group of designers from Kolding School of Design, Denmark, the complex responsibility of designing for on-going use is trialled in practice. Taking a critique of image-based design as a challenge: 'You get work through getting awards and the award system is based on photographs. Not use. Not context. Just purely visual photographs taken before people start using a [piece]',[11] *Daymaker Jacket* uses a system of layered, shifting lapels, to create a garment, the form of which changes through manipulation. The designers worked to create a piece that comes into its own as it is used and for this process of transformation to define the garment itself.

In a different project again, *A Timeless Ride*, a design team again from Kolding School of Design, investigates the unfolding of life

A Timeless Ride by Lin Borchersen Hansen, Anne Ditte Grøngaard
and Agnes Toksvig Bjerre

between and within layers of cloth and seam. Starting from an idea
of an active fashion object, grounded in the whirring of real life and
all its social and political significance, they asked what happens when
clothes are designed for movement, not just for sitting still? What if we
sketch, design, create not just objects but the actual, active use of those
things? Lin, Anne and Agnes explored articulation of joints, ventilating
layers, reflective details including knitted cuffs within pieces designed
for cycling. Here use is linked to movement of the body; to social
structures which influence how we choose to travel; and to the
mental patterns and knowledge that help us act in the world.

Slack space, loose fit

Other clues as to how to proceed can be found elsewhere. Jeremy Till,
in his book *Architecture Depends*, argues for the inclusion of 'slack space'
within design in order to accommodate changing times and situations
and to allow difference and ambiguity to thrive. He advocates design
that is 'conceptually unfinished to allow time to take its course'[12]
and for a loosening of control over design outcomes. 'Slack spaces',
he suggests, are, 'open to changing use – not literal flexibility … but
in terms of providing a frame for life to unfold within. It is space that
something will happen in, but exactly what that something might
be is not determinedly programmed. Slack space operates as a robust
background rather than a refined foreground … quietly setting a social
scene, not noisily constructing a visual sceneography … If slack space
is to be seen in time, it has to take what time throws at it. Welcoming
life into its interstices and not expelling it from shiny surfaces'.[13] And
so the design of unknown futures invokes new design practices and
changing business challenges geared towards collaboratively amplifying
the practices of use. This process where we design for a series of
dynamic interactions over time is perhaps what Bill Moggeridge
refers to when he says, 'we are designing verbs, not nouns'.[14]

Describing a more literal, material version of slack space as 'loose fit',
Stewart Brand, again writing about the built environment, in his title
How Buildings Learn, encourages design for adaptive use. For Brand,
this means physical change of the building itself over time with
maintenance playing a key role. 'Maintenance' he states, 'is learning':[15]

the fostering of informal, casual, astute and applied knowhow derived from actual experience of a particular space. Brand argues that this 'vernacular' knowledge be the foundation of design, finding form through diverse, small-scale projects, attuned to contradictions in order to extend a building's life. He observes that, 'Buildings do better over time when they are closely held and closely cared for',[16] revealing on-going use as active, hands-on tending directed by many things, including feelings, and which keep people at the centre of the idea.

Different clues again can be found in another construction and planning text, the iconic *A Pattern Language*. In it, Christopher Alexander and colleagues[17] extol the idea that designed things will not come alive unless they are 'made' by all those involved with them, and communicated by a common language that is also alive. Here a shared framework for working through practical solutions is offered, but within it, flexibility to adapt endlessly to preferences, needs, local conditions. The evolving 'pattern language' inveighs against other design languages that, 'are so brutal, and so fragmented … not based on human, or natural considerations',[18] instead offering a shared means of communication, and a source of joyful power, to talk in more holistic terms about what is good for people, about what needs to be done.

The paying heed

Ideas about designing for on-going use in which exchange between participants is an opportunity for empathy, insight and innovation can also be uncovered outside of architecture and planning. Poet Kathleen Jamie calls for, 'the care and maintenance of our web of noticing, the paying heed',[19] that is, a heightening of our powers of attention, honed on what is around us, a type of honouring. When we direct attention to moments and actions of on-going use, we pool energy around them: by noticing the many ordinary and sometimes extraordinary practices that go on with fashion in the context of its use, it fosters more of the same. We learn that reward is based in the use of what is around us, not just in consumption. No doubt 'the paying heed' would be classed as 'quiet sustainability',[20] far off the radar of corporate responsibility departments. It is also modest sustainability, readily understood and within the reach of us all, radiating out from individual actions, darning a hole, choosing to keep wearing what we already have. Indeed this type of quiet, bottom-up approach to change is rarely realised in association with brands and designers. And yet good design, which leads us towards new understanding, often starts with the divergent, expansive practices of the real world. As Tim Brown states: 'Good design thinkers observe. Great design thinkers observe the ordinary'.[21] Slack space, the paying heed, the craft of use is not at the centre of the fashion sector priorities and it is for this reason that designers and business leaders need to head there. Persuasive insights for new ways of doing things come from 'looking outward, to the edges of the market'.[22]

I was once asked at the end of the talk about how I imagined craft of use ideas and practices could be scaled up and shared more widely – the subtext of the question being about how could they fit within industry. At the time I answered that scaling them *out* was what was needed, replicating them in other places, for I didn't know if these things could or should be scaled up using market mechanisms and industrial logic. The questioner told me later that he was disappointed with my answer; and he restated his desire to know how the craft of use movement would fit in with business. Today still, questions of industry, scale and how these relate to practices of use are characterised by tension rather than easy answers. But today I would say something more and supplement my answer with a question. I see the craft of use and industry as mutually interdependent. They are in a reciprocal relationship, the presence of one impacting on the other, inevitably both will change. I would ask not how one could alter to fit within a larger one that remains unchanged, but how, going forward, both will shift. How could fashion business activity fit within the craft of use?

There was something else in his question that I agreed with then and still do today: an impatience for change, a desire to get to the point, to take action and to do this at speed and scale, something business and capitalism is particularly proficient at. This is essential, but this fast, big work also needs to be deep. It is second order, even third order change[23] that alters not just what we do, but also the way we think about what needs to happen in order to avoid replicating past problems. It finds opportunities for commercial practice in relationship with the life- and use-world of fashion.

The stories of 'garment co-operation'

Some garments require a wearer's involvement for them to work well on the body. Others act altogether differently and mould themselves around our frames and the actions of our lives. Such pieces remind us that garments and users are in dialogue; that clothes aid and abet and shape our world.

Portable pockets

I call these portable pockets. For a girl on the go, such as, myself ... I could put anything in these pockets. I have tape, I put my watercolours and my brushes, I can fit my sketchpad in here. I love this because I can wear it over jeans but I can also wear it over a dress and it looks great and it's made with a minimal amount of fabric ... I love how functional it is ... they're deep pockets ...

Marin City, USA, 2012

Sari lesson

This is the piece [in which] I actually learned how to tie a sari.
Dressing in a sari is always something that you preferably do
in front of a full-length mirror with an army involved (laughs).
And I always relied on either my mom or my sister ... There
was this one day that I was running late to go somewhere
and they said 'You know what? This time you are on your own.
Do it'. So two and a half hours later I showed up at the place
(laughs). And of course there are little things that you do
need help with, to see if the pleats are right ... but for the most
part, I was up and walking in it, and it didn't fall off as soon
as I stood. Saris make you stand up [straight] for sure. And you
definitely put on heels ... you need the extension, and it makes
it more elegant when it's draped down. I think it gives you a lot
of confidence, and I think that one of the things with the sari
is that for the most part it's a forgiving garment. And flattering.
So you can be pretty much any size and just carry it off well,
as long as you can carry yourself in it.

Vancouver, Canada, 2013

Cut to contours

This dress I got from a Swiss designer (Ida Gut) … she
is very good at making cuts for different types of bodies …
an organic kind of cutting that follows the muscles … I like
that I can feel on my body the change of material, it is nice
when you can feel a little pressure on the body, it gives you
kind of, I don't know, security like when somebody is holding
you know around your waist.

Kolding, Denmark, 2012

Careful removal

This jacket has been around for a really long time. I got it
when I just got out of high school. And it was that jacket which
makes you feel you look old and like professional and it's like
you would wear it for a job interview but then it just became
a part of my sort of regular winter rotation.

   I wore [it] so much that the lining was totally shredded on
the inside and it got to the point when I was embarrassed to
take it off in front of people because it was so trashed on the
inside. So I always took it off very carefully … I would make
sure that I was facing away, and then fold it over the chair to
hide the big shredded lining. I would never, just shrug it off
onto a chair that I was sitting on [inside-out], I would never
do that! Because if I stood up, you could see everything!
I was totally conscious of it …

Vancouver, Canada, 2013

Wear according to my life

For me usually things modify through wear rather than
me manipulating that modification. So, over time they'll
wear according to my life. My body. And putting too much
stuff in the pockets …

London, UK, 2012

A progressive broadening

Stories like those themed under banners of 'garment co-operation' and 'open and adjust' reveal surprise and unpredictability in the lives of garments. They show garments' dynamism, their vibrant force[24] and portray fashion as a world of constantly changing associations of fibre, colour, silhouette, skills, bodily actions, ideas and experiences. These multiple sources of action, some human, some not, respond in real time to each other, altering outcomes, influencing the whole.[25] Perhaps these stories capture fashion experiences where the division between object and subject, between garments and we, their users, dissolve. Perhaps they show us in relationship with many non-human forces that need us to, 'listen and respond more carefully to their outbreaks, objections, testimonies and propositions'.[26]

This holistic frame brings us back full circle to the experience of matter in motion, birds in flocks, garments in wardrobes, as part of life at the start of this chapter, and the deeper understanding that it affords. The stories of use of clothes suggest that garments have wisdom about them. The question is whether we are able to recognise it. And whether maybe the sustained attention we give to clothes through practices of use might help nurture these skills of noticing? Certainly the evidence of the *Local Wisdom* stories suggests that through the context of use we can know garments differently and as part of our common world.

Home economics and phenomenology

Such knowledge sits between conventional sector structures and traditional disciplinary knowledge. In these in–between, oftentimes slightly awkward, spaces, our challenge is to ask ever-deeper questions. Some of these questions are about overarching structures and ways of knowing. They are about ecology, ethics, economics, society, culture, engineering, psychology. Others are intensely practical. They are about hard skills: about seam construction, fit, laundering; about laying out a pattern, defuzzing a jumper, organising the sharing of a dress between you and your mates. Other questions combine hard with soft: how to develop an idea for what you want to do with your garment, how to enact it, how to develop the personal confidence to carry it through.

This hybrid knowledge is necessarily the new bread and butter activity of fashion and sustainability. In it we will draw on wonderful knowledge as varied as home economics, the applied study of managing resources in the household and family to improve the quality of everyday life; and phenomenology and Marcel Merleau-Ponty's thrilling work about the inseparability of mind and body, of us and the world, and the role that sensory perception plays in our understanding of it.[27] For Merleau-Ponty the world was not the unchanging object presented by the natural sciences, but instead endlessly relational, experienced direct and personal through our bodies. So it seems that the craft of use – an alliance between the vital forces of garments and bodies and brains through time – can, by following Merleau-Ponty's lead, become a route into the world, a way of deepening our experience of it, a process of animating the fashion system with a broad concern for others. And in so doing, changing it, retuning it to dance in rhythm with a new ethic.

A few years ago I was invited to speak at the annual conference of the International Federation for Home Economics. I was happy for the invitation. I was even happier amongst the delegates discovering how many the threads of similar ambition there were between us, between their work and mine. There are natural alliances everywhere, home and industry ecologies of practice waiting to be connected. What it means to know about fashion and sustainability is rightly changing as we begin to understand more about the limitations of information isolated from the details and dynamics of the whole fashion system; and begin to train our gaze beyond either industry producers or individual consumers as the main agents of change. In embracing on-going use of fashion through time, other possibilities emerge.

The stories of 'easy repair'

The fashion industry's industrial cut and sew techniques
produce an increasingly polished garment, so polished
in fact that it seems complete as is, closed to improvisation
from the 'outside'. But the design and construction of some
garments are different, more like a work in progress, open
to adaptation and repair and to building understanding
about how things are made.

Mismatch buttons

This is a chambray shirt and I took off all the buttons
and replaced them. I have jars and jars of antique buttons.
So I did a bunch of totally mismatched buttons. It's not the
most original idea … there's a project of a carpet maker …
who designs carpet tiles that are purposely mismatched, so
that if you stain one of the tiles and have to replace it, you
won't notice that it's been replaced because all the tiles are
mismatched anyway. So I thought, if I lose a button on the
shirt, you need to have a matching button unless you purposely
mismatch all of them, so that was the plan with this shirt.

San Francisco, USA, 2012

Raw edges endorse repair

This is one of my favourite sweaters made by a friend of mine
Nina French. She collects old sweaters from all over the world.
First she boils [them], then cuts them up and pieces them
together. There are no two that are alike. And when it does
fall apart occasionally, I sew it back up with different thread …
Here's a 1960s' ski sweater, here's a men's sweater; each of this
has the hand of many women.

Marin City, USA, 2012

Homemade

This dress I got in a thrift shop and somebody sewed it at home. It had a bunch of rips and things in it so I took it home and put a new zipper in it and ... because it's homemade ... if anything rips, if any seam tears it is so much easier to fix because it's not over-locked or anything. It fits me absolutely perfectly and I love it.

London, UK, 2010

4

Attentiveness, Materials, and Their Use

The Stories of Never Washed, Perfect Piece and My Community

Data on the levels of contemporary consumption of fashion garments
are startling. In 2012, average annual spending on clothing per UK
household was £1700.[1] Since then, UK consumer expenditure on
clothing and footwear has increased further: 0.6% in 2013 and 9.3%
in 2014.[2] Worldwide, rates of spending on clothes show a similar
trend. Inflation-adjusted figures for global expenditure on clothing
have increased 45% between 2006 and 2013 to US$460 billion.[3] And
in that same time the general trajectory of the price of clothing has been
downward.[4] We buy more; it costs less. Yet even amidst material excess,
it seems that our problem, to borrow from cultural critic Raymond
Williams, is that we are not materialistic enough.[5] We see little intrinsic
value in material goods and their qualities. We don't know how things
are made, having little idea how they work as they do. We can't tell one
fibre from another by a quick appraising rub between finger and thumb.
We don't know a material or fabric construction by its hand and lustre.
We don't look for and appreciate – or even know about – the fine detail
in a garment. We don't revere the things we already have.

The philosopher Alain de Botton explains the dynamics of the
situation: 'Two centuries ago, our forebears would have known the
precise history and origin of nearly every one of the limited number
of things they ate and owned, as well as of the people and tools involved
in their production ... The range of items available for purchase may
have grown exponentially since then, but our understanding of their
genesis has diminished almost to the point of obscurity. We are now
as imaginatively disconnected from the manufacturing and distribution
of our goods as we are practically in reach of them'.[6]

Contemporary consumer culture, permeated with a pressure for
newness and perfection, is characterised by a process of alienation
from the items – the garments – we have in large numbers. It seems,
in Richard Sennett's words that, 'modern society is de-skilling people
in the conduct of daily life'.[7] In it we experience a disconnection from

supply chains, material and manufacturing processes, from time frames and geographies, and contexts of use. Albert Borgmann calls this process of alienation with the material environment 'user disburdenment',[8] a process he places at the centre of technological culture. User disburdenment seems also to symbolise fashion culture, which is increasingly dominated by brands and sign making, over material making,[9] and in which we are becoming less cognisant of the detail and knowledge of how garments 'work' and less challenged into awareness of our use of them. According to Matthew Crawford, that modern society presents us with fewer occasions to exercise our judgement – to practice the virtue of 'judging things rightly' – damages human culture.[10] Borgmann expands this point, arguing that a failure to catch our awareness by actively engaging with things undermines the development of our sensitivity to ethical responsibility. Instead he advocates a design process to create objects that, 'still involves some pain to use, some work. By being less than completely polite, somewhat drawing attention to itself, its materiality and its design, such a thing would enable ethical ways of being'.[11]

True materialism

The enabling of ethical ways of being through engagement with the material world, polite or not, is at the core of what has been described as 'true' or 'new' materialism and its heightened sense of both the limits and potential of the material world. It suggests that through fostering a deep appreciation and respect for intrinsic material qualities of things we develop an understanding of their value in ways that go beyond their usefulness to us. Charged by this knowledge, we act with care.

In the consumer society, much material consumption is driven by a search for social meaning or symbolic value. Fashion is an archetypal sign economy, where non-material meanings fuel purchase of material goods. In a sign economy, where people crave images and social meaning, a good's materiality becomes less important, pieces are not valued for their intrinsic qualities, but they are no less in demand. When it is sign values that count and the signs deemed meaningful change (symbols are highly susceptible to the dynamics of rapidly changing trends), replacement purchases of material goods become

necessary.[12] Here true materialism offers a change of direction:
a switch from an idea of a consumer society where materials matter
little, to a truly material society, where materials – and the world
they rely on – are cherished.

Some of this more truly material ground is trodden by the ideas
and practices of the craft of use. It isn't necessarily easy or attractive
knowledge that we amass as we use clothes, but at least it will be *our*
understanding and awareness garnered from handling, tending and
wearing *our* fashion pieces. There's a certain amount of personal
bravery required to gain this understanding, for we need to trust our
own instincts and judgement about the things we have in front of us.
We have to overcome the fear (after Thoreau's *Walden* and the story
of the *Broken Pantaloon*, p.250) that showing ourselves in the same,
well-worn clothes is worse than weak moral character. Could a pair
of hands and eyes that have close involvement with and appreciate
the potential inherent with a garment, help us to make choices that
maintain us within material limits? Could a love for garments transform
us into lovers of the constraints of the broader world? I wonder if these
relationships can be summarised, albeit crudely, like this:

> Have lots of them – don't know them.
> Know them – enjoy them, be charmed or frustrated by them,
> love them, change them, understand them.
> Understand them – demand them less.

Material choices and the craft of use

Throughout the process of gathering the stories for the craft of use
project, I kept a highly unscientific, back-of-the-napkin tally of the
general categories of garments and fibre types brought along to the
community photo shoots. The range of garment types was, predictably,
vast, with the best-represented single items being T-shirts followed
by denim pieces, jeans in particular. It seems perhaps that the language
of use is spoken and heard most often in jeans and T-shirts: they
are 'work horses' of many people's wardrobes. Certainly in the
case of denim jeans, they lend themselves to conspicuous display of
being worn; their surface an embodied, often pleasing record of use.

A T-shirt's single jersey fabric doesn't gather a surface patina in the same way as denim, nonetheless for many it seems to act as a ready canvas on which we can write our own histories. Perhaps it is the ubiquity and frequent use of T-shirts and jeans that lends them to figure strongly in our imagination of use of fashion; and this normalcy and accessibility is their power. They are not too special to save for special occasions. They are not too precious to try a hand at fixing or altering, at experimenting with (though neither are the most straightforward to alter). They are an invitation for wear; all-purpose, quietly charismatic, friendly.

My impressionistic tally of the fibre types represented in the stories also revealed an almost overwhelming preference for natural materials. It seems that garments in natural fibres are more 'obvious' to people asked about practices and the context of use of fashion. Perhaps they are more 'cared for' in use, more high maintenance even, than pieces made in synthetic fibres and so are reported on differently. Cotton fibres were the single best-represented material type in the garment stories, but this was closely followed by pieces made from wool. Together, tales of active, on-going use of garments made from cotton and wool dwarfed completely the total number of stories involving pieces made in all other fibres. In the global fibre market, cotton commands a 28.4% share,[13] which perhaps goes some way to explaining its frequency of the craft of use stories. But wool is a minority fibre, accounting for 1.3% of global trade,[14] suggesting perhaps that garments made from wool are used, and viewed, differently to those made from other fibres, an insight worthy of further exploration. The life-worlds of woollen pieces appear unlike those of garments created out of other fibre types.

Another minority fibre, silk, also features surprisingly often in stories of use of fashion, particularly given how little silk is sold on international textile markets (0.2%).[15] Perhaps silk's status as a fibre of high value and refinement translates into a qualification for on-going use? If this were the case, this might offer one explanation as to why synthetic fibres were represented barely at all in the stories: their perceived low value both monetarily and as a cultural currency.

The scant representation of synthetic fibres in the stories also raises an uncomfortable question about what is happening to polyester – the

'A twofold relationship between on-going use of fashion
and a garment's materiality is best understood in the round'

world's most ubiquitously traded fibre (52.2% of global total)[16] – when, in clothing form, it enters homes and lives, as it seems to play a limited part in people's ideas and experiences of satisfying use.

Also uncovered by the craft of use stories is a twofold relationship between on-going use of fashion and a garment's materiality, a relationship that is best understood in the round. One part of this relationship is an obvious physical link between the design, material, construction and cut of some garments and the use practices that follow. Here materiality is an active, tangible shaping force that invites certain things to happen with clothes in people's lives; that scripts some behaviours of use, albeit imperfectly.

The limits to this force are legion, dependent on everything from an individual's haptic skill to collective cultural norms, and include among other things, our attentiveness, imagination and the amount of money in our pocket. The conclusion: materials shape things and they don't shape everything; yet they still contain power, are basic to the actions that follow, are folded into a bigger whole. This bigger whole, the second part of the relationship between the materiality of fashion and its associated use practices, is less direct. Here a garment's materiality is an enabling presence for action, a platform on which the habits of mind and capabilities of a self-reliant individual can be developed, with clothes and life as the context. Fashion and fibre becomes the tool by which we practice the skills of – to use John Ehrenfeld's evocative term – flourishing.[17]

Materiality and laundering practices

The stories clustered under the heading of 'never washed' exemplify this twofold relationship. In some cases materials are revealed as the things that influence actions directly; the intrinsic characteristics of fibre, fabric, colour and garment cut, leading and shaping how we choose to launder a piece. And in other cases, materials and the garments they are made into are cast in a completely different, supporting role, where they enable us to carry through a particular idea, decision or sentiment around laundering practices, but they themselves don't presage it.

Wool, and particularly woollen knitwear, features heavily in examples of garments that have never been laundered, an observation that probably tallies with many of our own experiences of laundry and the pieces that are washed more and less frequently. It also, happily, chimes with the fibre's actual properties that support infrequent or no washing: a complex, scaly fibre structure that gives wool durability, bulk, elasticity, moisture absorption and release, a degree of natural stain resistance and the ability to shrink if agitated when wet.[18] Many of these properties seem to percolate in the minds of the people who never wash woollen clothes, carrying forward what they know about the affordances of the fibre into their subsequent actions. Wool, for instance, 'allows' them to not launder a garment because its stain resistance properties means it never really gets 'dirty enough' to warrant laundering, justifying their decision not to bother washing it (*Lazy* p. 151), for others still, the fibre bulk and the natural variation of colour (when undyed), makes dirt hard to see, and so makes washing, to get rid of visible stains at least, unnecessary.

In some of the 'never washed' stories, wool's properties in the physical realm are augmented as holders of meaning and memories – and together fibre and sentiment influence the practices of use. In these stories, laundering was delayed because of a concern that soap and water would 'wash away' emotional connections and its somatic triggers, often a scent (*Preservation* p. 157) but sometimes visible stains (*Coffee + laughter* p. 149) and because of wool's propensity to shrink if not laundered correctly, washing could mean that both the garment and the memory would be lost. Indeed a notion that laundering somehow strips away or spoils something of value in clothes, pops up time and again, altering, to some extent, the behaviours that follow. If an item contains a lot of delicate handwork, beading or embroidery for example, then laundering might be avoided because of a fear that washing would damage it (*Honour the handwork*, p. 158). Here a garment's materiality stretches out to influence the subsequent use-world of the garment.

Yet despite these examples, the path of direct and singular influence of a garment's materiality, design and construction on the practices of use is unpredictable, hard to plan for. For instance, in order for a garment's materiality to communicate no laundering, a user first has to read the material cues accurately (to identify the piece, say, as wool, or of delicate construction, etc.); then to know what that means for its use and upkeep; and further to act on this knowledge accordingly, perhaps breaking routines and habitualised behaviour or flying in the face of cultural taboos in the process. Certainly this does happen. But other types of garment use practices which result in no laundering happen also and start from an idea or human agency, not materials. By, say, avoiding wearing a piece in direct contact with the skin (and assuming that ridding a garment of bodily dirt and odour is seen as a chief reason for washing it), then laundering becomes unnecessary (*Underlay*, p.150). Other reasons for not laundering are more ideological: a punk's denim jacket, a symbol of counter-cultural intent, is never cleaned lest it endorse the norms of the very culture it is trying to rail against (*Anti-establishment*, p.148).

Others still, and perhaps my personal favourites, tell that some amongst us simply don't care about a few stains on their clothes and continue to wear the pieces regardless (*No one sees the stains*, p.154; *Just a few stains*, p.159). The garment's materiality stands in visible defiance of social conditioning; the wearer shrugs off the pressure to be shiny, unmarked and 'as new' (*I like it as it is*, p.152). It seems to me that this capacity – a lovely, burgeoning self-reliance, where the user creates their own path, including through their fashion choices – is the craft of use. It is part material object, part idea, part story, part knowledge, part skills, part individual, part collective structure, irreducible to a single element.

The stories of 'never washed'

Laundering is high impact and yet not laundering is socially
unacceptable. But some pieces defy social pressure and are
never washed, often motivated by the fear that laundering
causes something precious to be lost: a scent, a memory,
the particular way a garment fits, its colour, the quality
of handwork, and even a political stance.

Anti-establishment

In 1978 my mum gave me £10 to buy a jacket and jeans
and this is the one I bought. Back then I was a punk and
I sewed badges on the back ... Sex Pistols, Sham 69, The
Stranglers ... and my grandad's RAF stripes on the arm.
I've still never washed it ... why would I?

Bollington, UK, 2009

Coffee + laughter

This jumper belonged to my mum in the 1970s. Her sister
knitted it. They're both deceased so this piece is very special
to me … I loved it as a child because it's really warm and cosy
and now what I particularly like about it is the coffee stains.
My mum was kind of an erratic laugher and you know, when
she would be drinking coffee she spilled it down it … she was
really upset but she had the week before, dipped her cuff into
a coffee and only a week later she had spilled all these little
coffee stains down the front. So I didn't want to wash them
out … not that I probably could 'cause it's probably like 20
years ago that she did that.

Dublin, Ireland, 2012

Underlay

This jean jacket I've never washed because I wear a hoody
underneath it … Maybe it gets dirty on the outside, kind
of worn … it doesn't really matter. But I will always wear
an under layer so I don't have to wash it.

San Francisco, USA, 2011

Lazy

It's just a dark blue woollen jumper and it was given to me by my girlfriend but I haven't got round to washing it yet 'cause it's 'hand wash only' and I'm a bit lazy and you know, wool is, is self-cleaning isn't it?

London, UK, 2010

I like it as it is

I've never washed this skirt because I haven't really needed
to … It's got a hole in it there as well; I hadn't noticed that, I'll
have to sew that up. I don't really want to wash it because I'm
worried that the sequins and things will come off, as some of
them have, but I quite like the fact that it's quite tatty as well.

London, UK, 2010

Oiled denim

I wear this vest [sleeveless jacket] very frequently. It's a raw denim – oiled raw denim – and it's got such a thickness and niceness to the fabric, and even though it's kind of a casual style, you can wear it anywhere and it kind of works over no sleeves or long sleeves. And it's got a nice neck; and buttoned up it keeps you very warm when you want to be warm. And I never have to wash it. It doesn't get dirty. It doesn't pick up smells at all. Like you can go into a smoke-filled bar and you don't even smell the cigarette smoke on it. It just takes wear very well. I've had it about 7 years so, and plan to have it at least that long again.

San Francisco, USA, 2011

No one sees the stains

This coat is a hand me down. I think it's been through many
people. A friend was trying to get rid of things. And I put
it on and I get compliments on it when I'm wearing it. But
it's covered in stains, which I find really funny because nobody
ever sees the stains. They're always thinking and saying, 'Oh
that colour is really nice' or 'that fits you really well'. But no
one ever says, 'oh look there is something spilled all over the
arm'. I'm not bothered by the stains. I think it's interesting
to wear things that kind of go against what you're supposed
to be wearing. And see how people respond to it and just
the fact that no one sees the stains.

New York, USA, 2013

Loose cut

This dress is from when I spent three weeks in the Sinai with
a Bedouin family and gave me this as a present. And this one
I never wash, because you do not really sweat in it … the cut
is so loose.

Kolding, Denmark, 2012

Weather cleaning

This is a traditional tweed jacket that my parents bought
for me during a holiday in Ireland about thirteen years
ago now ... I've never washed it – I wear it in the rain.

London, UK, 2012

Preservation

I inherited this jumper from my father-in-law and call it
'the camping jumper' as it always comes with us on holiday.
It's the thing I throw on at night to keep warm. I've never
washed it … I'm afraid it would shrink. I've shrunk a lot of
things over the years. It would also lose its fantastic smell –
a mix of fresh air and wood smoke.

Bollington, UK, 2009

Honour the handwork

This is my sequined cardigan that has never been washed …
I'd be scared to ruin it. Like, it's all hand-beaded, I just think
the amount I wear it and the amount of time it spends sort
of hung up, it doesn't really warrant washing it, you know,
I wear it and then it gets to air for, like, six months before
I wear it again.

London, UK, 2010

Just a few stains

This jacket has been in my family only for about ten years now.
My mother purchased it … and as you can see there are a few
stains on it she was unable to remove. The garment itself is just
beautiful in my opinion. It's well-made, it's a very interesting
fabric, it has a lot of interesting details. The way you put it's sort
of almost like origami-esque … There's a wraparound belt that
hinges in the back that almost makes it more of a shirt because
it's impractical to take it on and off and … the bow itself is on
the shoulder [and] can come off so I've worn this in my hair so
there's multi uses for it. [My mother] was ready to throw it out
but I snatched it up before she was able to do that and I wear it,
even though there are a few stains. For me, it doesn't bother me
one bit so I still wear the garment … if it's dark no one can see
the stains, right? It's part of her wardrobe that is now part of
my wardrobe, serving the same purpose …

San Francisco, USA, 2011

Materiality and ideal fashion pieces

The complex and idiosyncratic relationship between a garment's materiality – that is its fibre type, construction details, its design and cut – and its use, is also visible in stories of garments that people self-identify as their ideal or perfect piece.

I have a pair of trousers that for me are perfect: high-waisted, easy fit, tailored narrow around the ankle with a turn up, faded soft grey-blue. I have mended them repeatedly: reinforced areas where the fabric is thinning; replaced a zip; shored up the hook and eye fastening on the waistband; stitched up the hems twice; even tried my grandmother's technique for ironing a semi-permeable crease down the front by running the edge of a bar of soap on the crease's reverse (it didn't work and just left a greasy line running down the leg). I've shinned up a tree in them, received an award in them; they are completely knackered. For many reasons we suit each other.

I am sure that other women who bought these same trousers also like them, but for me, in the unique conditions of my life, they are ideal. Here, a confederation of forces, material and immaterial, combine to create the conditions for satisfying use. The craft of use stories assembled under the theme of 'perfect piece' give up many clues as to these forces and their relationships. Predictably, it's not a simple solution they offer; perhaps the only common detail they share is that these pieces have been in wardrobes for years. It seems then an appreciation of a garment's perfect suitability, keeps these things alive. The value of a piece is sometimes augmented by its price (*A cashmere tale*, p. 166) and sometimes not – made more special by discovering it on the floor (*Fell into my path*, p. 167). Other stories find perfection in a garment's ability to fit everyone (*Fits all owners perfectly*, p. 169) or by contrast, just one body well (*Body changer*, p. 163). Some of them need no adjustment (*Daily shawl*, p. 168) and others much tinkering within their ideal structure to make them 'right' (*Aptness comes in many forms*, p. 164). Running through quite a few of the tales was a concern about what would happen when the piece had worn out; could it, should it, be remade? And how would that be negotiated?

'In the unique conditions of my life they are ideal'

The stories of 'perfect piece'

Consumerist fashion is all about what is right on trend,
right for uniform mass-manufacture and ultimately right
for the figures on a balance sheet. Lost in the mix are a
garment's finesse, fit, appropriateness; and the space to
nurture individuality, skills and confidence in a wearer
to recognise and revel in the 'rightness' of a particular piece.
   Finding the right partnership between wearer and
garment is the difference between using a piece time
and again or throwing it away. Each partnership, like
each person, is different. Matching one with the other and
being open to the almost limitless variety of possibilities
this enables, underscores fashion system diversity.

Body changer

I purchased the shirt I'm wearing second hand in Portland.
I bought it because I couldn't understand how it would be
worn when I saw it hanging on the hanger … It intrigued
me in its construction and when I put it on I liked the way
that it actually changed my body shape … It's quite shapeless
and when you put it on it actually makes you look about 10
pounds thinner. Woohoo! It's very soft. It's very comfortable
and when it wears out I intend to copy it. It's so easy to wear.

San Francisco, USA, 2011

Aptness comes in many forms

This is a coat that I love that a friend gave me. I think the
label is Product. I can't find this designer anywhere. I'm actually
just going to have to go to a tailor with this coat and ask her
to recreate it in another fabric of her choice.

    I love this coat like I love few other garments but it is
absolutely shot. I've used it for years ... I love the drape and
I love that it's very light and it's still pretty windproof. Friends
have said, 'Oh you look so French today'. I know what they're
trying to say but I don't think this looks like an especially
French garment. I think they're saying that there's something
unusual about the coat. I share that belief.

    The arms are too short. I don't know why because I don't
think I have especially long arms. It's the one thing I don't like.
So when I have it remade in Brooklyn, the arms will be longer
and while we're at it the buttons need to come down further ...
The buttons only come to about navel length and you know
wind blows it open. I don't want to judge. I don't know what
the idea was for the design ending at the belly, but that's it.
Other than that, perfect.

New York, USA, 2013

Recognise a garment's rightness

This is a vintage skirt from the 70s. When I want something really special, I raid charity shops looking for vintage things, particularly skirts and blouses, because they're cut quite traditionally and they suit my figure.

Bollington, UK, 2009

A cashmere tale

This coat is the piece-de-resistance in my wardrobe in that it's probably, you know, the most high quality coat that I have ever put on my back and I'd never be able to afford to buy it. The history of this coat is that it was bought to be worn in a Shakespeare play – the production of 'The Winter's Tale'. I went to see the dress rehearsal of this show ... and on [the actor] walked in this coat and I thought; 'that is just the most beautiful coat in the world'. And the show played for two months I guess, probably about 50 performances so the coat had to do its stuff. It had to get worn and it had to be robust enough and that's why they bought a £1200 cashmere coat for her to wear.

   When the show was coming to an end, I went to the wardrobes department and I said 'what are you going to do with that coat?' and they said, 'oh, don't know, it'll probably go into storage', and I said, 'well, if you feel like selling it I'll buy it' ... About 5 years after I bought it I went to a party and there was the actress who wore it in the show and she said, 'did you buy that coat that I had in Winter's Tale?', 'Have you still got it?' and I said, 'yes, it's upstairs hanging up on the rail' and she said, 'oh, can I go up and try it on again?' So we trouped up the stairs in the middle of this party and stood in front of the mirror in the bedroom where the coats were while she tried it on again. It had stayed in her mind exactly as it did in mine.

London, UK, 2011

Fell into my path

I'm wearing my pink sweater and I found it on the ground
at my best friend's art opening when we were walking around
outside afterward. I was sixteen when I found it so I've had
it for seven years now and it's still my favourite sweater. It
fits me perfectly and is my favourite colour, the kind of thing
that I would have tried really hard to locate in a store but
just literally fell into my path and I've worn [it] ever since.

San Francisco, USA, 2011

Daily shawl

This shawl is woven by a very small Irish weaving company.
They actually design in Ireland but they produce them in
Germany – but they do say hand woven in Ireland on it (laughs)
but they're very much Irish-based. It's one hundred percent
pure wool and I've had it for over ten years. And I honestly
wear it almost every single day, I'm not joking. I wear it all
the time. And I wear it going out, I wear it in, I lend it to people
in the house. I don't really give it to anyone to bring away. But
I give it to people to stay warm when they're visiting or if they
need it. And it still looks completely almost the same as it did
the first day I got it – I didn't actually get it, my parents gave
it to a boyfriend of mine at the time and when we split up
I took it (laughs).

Dublin, Ireland, 2012

Fits all owners perfectly

This dress was bought from an op shop for my sister by
her best friend, years and years ago. And her mom altered
it by hand to fit my sister perfectly.

    And she wore it for a number of years but, because it
is so old, it is slowly disintegrating, tearing at the seams
and that sort of thing. My sister has no real skill in altering
or fixing clothes at all, so she just cast it off to me and said,
'I can't wear this, it's falling apart to shreds,' even though
it fitted her immaculately. On me it was just a bit tight and
uncomfortable and so I pulled apart all the hand-sewing
that had been done and now it fits me perfectly … You
know it seems to have fitted everyone perfectly that's owned
it. A lot of it has been done by hand and there's no overlocking.
It's all French seamed. You'd think it was made at home but it
has a tag on it though no care label or anything. So I think it has
just been altered and altered and altered.

    But I ironed it last night for the first time since I've owned
it. And just everytime that I looked at something, there is some
little alteration that has been done, so it just feels like a constant
work in progress to be the perfect fit for whoever owns it.

Wellington, New Zealand, 2013

Use = materiality + people + time + space

The evidence of the 'perfect piece' stories settles and pools around
an idea that is larger and more slippery than is quickly manageable:
what matters for the use of clothes is a garment's materiality plus
people plus time plus space. An equation with a sum that is different
each time we tot it up, because the variables are always in flux. The
significance and role played by materials shifts depending on who
is involved, where their head is at, what their hands can do and what
their friends are thinking. If we are to work with the insight of the
craft of use stories, the task ahead is to resist reducing their wisdom
to simpler parts – to, say, not focus only on materials, often the
place where many sustainability conversations begin – and instead
to deal with whole, to actively work with all parts and in open
acknowledgement of the interconnected forces between them.
This might mean we work to foster attitudes and preferences that
find familiar garments, special, beautiful, radical. To sketch out
possible surroundings or conditions in which the experience of a
perfect garment helps us find satisfaction – even satiation – in other
existing pieces. To prototype materials, colour palettes, construction
and cut within bigger stories of relationships.

 Some of these ideas were explored in design work that accompanied
the gathering of stories and portrait shots. A group project at
Massey University, New Zealand, queried what happens if the users
of clothing were the ones to say from what, why and when a garment
gets made? And more than that, who it is for? In the *Doppelgänger
Project*, individuals were asked to pick a piece that they felt had a
good 'genotype', a garment whose blueprint satisfies. Building on
the thought that no matter how perfectly suited to us a piece is,
there are always elements that we might wish to change, Doppelgänger
asked the user about ways it could be evolved to improve it further.
This in-vivo, in-wardrobe, product development process tried to capture
not only the genetic code (the 'spirit') of an already successful garment
but also to grow it in line with the hard won experience of using the
piece in a material, social world. The garment 'child' was then gifted
to someone of the original owner's choosing. The DNA recombined
and passed on.

Doppelgänger Project by Alex Barton, Monica Buchan-Ng and Katie Collier

Materials and community in fashion

The nuanced relationship between design, fibre, fabric and garment and the fashion use practices that follow is further teased apart through stories that say something about the relationship between how we use fashion, and ideas or values of community. In the category of stories entitled 'my community', the power of a garment's materiality to ground people in place, to signal particular values, to connect us with others, is clear. Colour, fibre and pattern shout out about origin and choice as the garment is created. Here it also seems that the visible signs of community in some pieces (see the stories of *Seasonal yellow*, p. 179 and *Patterns of the islands*, p. 174) act as a constant reminder of difference in a garment, and perhaps a spur also to go on to use it differently.

Yet 'a pattern language' (to borrow Christopher Alexander's wonderful phrase)[19] of community-inspired usership is also spoken and shown in ways beyond materials. Here economic opportunity (*British wear*, p. 176), local creativity and pride (*Brooklyn geometry*, p. 175), shared values (*Social entrepreneur*, p. 177), community as an incubator for growing long-lasting understanding (*Jobs for the people*, p. 178) become apparent. And so the practices of use become trusted vehicles for a wide variety of personal and political change.

The stories of 'my community'

In smaller communities people can more easily see
the effects of their own actions on each other and
the environment. They can also better understand
the ramifications of their choices; enabling them to
take responsibility for them. Expressing community
through our garment choices sews the seeds of a new
type of fashion interdependence based on connection
to people and place.

Pattern of the islands

This is a very precious garment. It was knitted for me by
my great aunt, my grandmother's cousin. She came from
the island of Tiree in the Inner Hebrides. My grandmother
lived with us when I was growing up, so I used to sit on her
lap as a child. And she would tell me the stories of my ancestors
who were fisherfolk on the Isle of Tiree and how the women,
who all had white hair in their late twenties … would sit on the
beaches and knit the patterns of the islands on the fishermen's
jerseys. But they were also waiting for their husbands to come
back. So there was a way of knitting, which she described …
with your needles tucked 'under your oxters' [armpits].
So they would knit from memory these patterns …
    So my great aunt came to live in New Zealand, a doctor,
retired in her sixties … and she asked me if I would like
a jumper and I told her the story that I remembered my
grandmother telling me, and she knitted those patterns
that she remembered from Tiree into this. I've had it for
twenty-five years and I've never washed it and I would
wear it some years, some not. Some years I wear it a lot …

Wellington, New Zealand, 2013

Brooklyn geometry

I am wearing a hoody. It's sort of a cobalt blue with various
geometric patterns on it. It's sewn from reclaimed sweater
materials. I love the sort of handmade, DIY quality of it.
I found a design team on the Internet that sells pants and
hoodies and sort of street wear done in bold, geometric
colours and they're based in Brooklyn. Everything good
comes from Brooklyn.

San Francisco, USA, 2011

British wear

The whole shebang [sic] is all made by young British designers,
mostly using British materials. From fox flannel and British
drill cotton … and this is Italian jersey, it's really super fine
but it's got metal woven into nylon tape … to give that sort of
nice effect. It looks fairly, sort of, normal but if the light shines
on it you look a little Graham Norton-esque but in a cool way
because it's nicely cut. My socks are Japanese but apart from
that everything I wear is British. Not in any sort of jingoistic
way but I like promoting young, British talent and I don't
think enough people do it.

London, UK, 2011

Social entrepreneur

This is my mum's old scarf that I grew up with. And these
are really well known scarves in Norway. Everyone who
was a Socialist or worked in teaching, education or something
political, they used those scarves in the 70s … [they] signified
people who were interested in creativity and social welfare.
[They were] made by a female entrepreneur in Norway called
Sigrun Berg … she saw that women had lost the grounding
for making money for their house[hold]. So she started people
to weave. She started selling cartloads and that's the way
a lot of people managed to keep their homes.

Oslo, Norway, 2011

Jobs for the people

This is a sweater of my mother's, from the fifties. It is the only piece that I have of hers. My mother used to own a clothing store, I grew up above the store … in the store, running around, trying on the hats (laughs). My mother was very influential on me … we were in a very small town in Canada, and I must have been seven or eight, when she gave me some money and said, 'You need to buy yourself some sneakers'. 'Go down the street and try to buy something Canadian if you can'. And that really stayed with me. And later I understood. What she was trying to do, she was in business, and she understood the importance of having jobs for people in the community …

Vancouver, Canada, 2013

Seasonal yellow

This is a piece I dyed with a seasonal weed that grows in
our neighbourhood and all over Northern California and
it's called Sourgrass or Oxalis. It's a really great colour to
work with because you don't need a mordant [to fix the dye
to the fibre], the mordant [Oxalic Acid] is actually in the plant
already. Oxalis shows up pretty much when the rains start
to come, like the end of November, and it stays until it starts
to get dry which is the end of April ... When it's gone it's
gone and you can't get it and you can't preserve it, so you
have to use that colour then. So it's truly the opposite of
seasons of fashion because you can't extract it on the industry
side. You have to wait for nature.

San Francisco, USA, 2011

5

Durability, Design and Enduring Use

The Stories of Super Long Life,
Patina of Use and Flexible Thinking

The painful, pressing reality of planetary boundaries confers limits
to production and consumption of fashion. It also confers an obligation
to experiment, as individuals and as an industry, with exuberance and
diversity to do more with the things we already have. Durability is an
essential part of a society with a different relationship to growth,[1] and
of the craft of use, for fundamental to the on-going use of a piece is
its 'lastingness'. Such lastingness may even work to slow consumption
of replacement items; by extending the potential for satisfaction with
existing pieces, no additional ones are required. New consumption
is forestalled, resources are saved, waste is reduced, needs are met.

Yet the relationship between enduring use and durability is
scrambled. The repeated use of things, like clothes, is dependent on
many factors. In the fashion context, a set of psycho-social factors render
a materials approach to durability a weak force in determining whether
something continues to be used. Many of the *Local Wisdom* stories
of garment use show that garments which defy obsolescence do so in
informal or unintentional ways, rarely as a result of design planning
or material or product qualities. What we see instead is that extended,
active use of fashion clothes emerges from strategies of human action
and intention: that things last and continue to be used when people
want them to. Durability, while facilitated by materials, design and
construction, is overseen by an altogether different vector of action;
by a social system that shapes an ideology of use.

Durability and sustainability

Over the last two decades durability has proven a recurring theme
within fashion and sustainability, including in design thinking and
practice, the area I know best. Much of the development work of
design for durability, such as that pioneered by the group *Eternally
Yours*,[2] was developed in product design and has, over the last decade,

migrated to fashion, where it has been appropriated both at a materials level and to influence product–user relationships. Limitations with these approaches are increasingly well understood, and chiefly rest on the effects of idiosyncratic user behaviour and structures of consumer culture influencing the success of durability strategies to shape consumption patterns. Expending resources and effort to extend the lives of products pays few dividends unless the users of those pieces take advantage of the benefits provided by their longer life – the extra days–weeks–years of use they provide – and further acts to slow consumption of new items and reduce the totalised throughput of resources.

The user-dependent – the *human-dependent* – nature of the factors that affect on-the-ground lifespans of products means that strategies that pursue durability as a way to influence consumption are full of contingencies and complexity. The incongruity of relying on *things* alone to influence *people's behaviour* to in turn foster longevity of those *things* is amplified in the context of garments by the deeply social nature of fashion: what one person chooses to wear, and to wear for a long time, is also affected by the decisions and actions of others.

Fashion and durability

In the fashion context, ideas about durability are tinged by additional politics. For some, it is challenging to reconcile long lasting garments with the very idea of fashion itself, or more particularly with a notion of fashion in thrall to its own frivolous, evanescent, ever-changing nature. On other scores too, ambiguity around durability is uncovered. Understood as an economic and cultural process, fashion seems to deny the possibility of a more durable material culture. For as 'a market-driven cycle of consumer desire and demand; and … a modern mechanism for the fabrication of the self',[3] fashion becomes a commercial force based on rapid product obsolescence and continually increasing throughput of resources. Joanne Finkelstein sets out this cycle's relentlessness, 'if we are relying upon the properties of procured goods for our sense of identity, then we are compelled to procure again and again'.[4]

Yet this view of fashion has not always held sway. Jutta Gronow reminds us that, 'originally fashion was not consciously created; it was born as a side-product of purposive social action'.[5] As I write this line I wonder, *Dear Reader*, whether perhaps it is both the time and the place to reclaim fashion in its original form as an expression of our activism? To, at the very least, begin to imagine action, not watching, or looking, as a powerful fashion currency. Certainly many of us already act with purpose in the social world. *Local Wisdom* stories nearly always unfold from a process of being active in some way: of manipulating fabric with fingers and thread, of having fun, of doing things with others. Consciously understanding fashion in action terms reveals (with the certainty afforded by experience) practices of garment use as a fundamental part of the fashion process. Users may be far away from fashion capitals. What we wear may be old hat. But it is part of the fashion whole all the same.

The whole features many long-lived, well-loved, intensely worn pieces, at least if the tales of use I recorded are anything to go by. The stories of 'super long life' are tales of durability in clothing that span many years and incarnations. Even though it is sometimes presumed that old things reach an advanced age because of an ability to resist changing external conditions, to tenaciously hold their shape, to be 'bomb-proof' (here old is read as unyielding, rigid, motionless, a site or object preserved in aspic, a place without dynamic change); in the stories of use I gathered, this was not the case. Durability was not an inert quality or experience. On the contrary, the stories reveal old age as lively. They uncover agedness as a beating heart animating a process of on-going change in both garment and the person wearing it, written through the passing of time.

The stories of 'super long life'

Making a garment last is very different to making a long-lasting garment. Enduring use is often difficult to predict. It is specific and personal, linked less with materials and more with ways of thinking, experiences and memories. Finding ways to access these may be critical to third, fourth or fifth lives.

Childhood to adult use

This was my jumper when I was seven. My mother bought it for me on an office trip overseas to Japan [when she went to] Tokyo Disneyland. And when she first purchased it for me I was too embarrassed to wear it because of the colour and the pictures.

So this was in a cupboard, hidden, lost for a very long time … but I wear it now. I'm not the same size [as I was when I was seven]. It's actually quite a bit shorter. But I think from laundering it somehow kind of stretches a little … I don't know I think because it's knit so I kind of get away with wearing it just a little too small … I didn't grow very much (laughs).

Melbourne, Australia, 2013

Four generations+

This jacket originally belonged to a second or third cousin
of mine; Anita Louise Erman. She passed away fairly young.
My grandmother ended up inheriting most of her physical
goods [and now] I take care of them and let other members
of my family continue to use them too. The jacket went from
Anita to Didi to Chris to Laurel.

   It was something they thought was important because
[it's] in really good condition … thought [to be] of value.
The jacket has Aunt Anita's initials inside. It's actually kind
of ironic because she died due to alcohol … I mean her
initials were A.L.E. It's sort of weird […] weird little thing.

San Francisco, USA, 2011

Durable trash

I wear this weird jumpsuit thing a lot and I inherited it
from my mum and she inherited from her grandma, so that's
my great grandma. So three generations in my family have
worn it. My great grandma bought it when she was going
on a package holiday to stay at the beach and do nothing …
a kind of trashy culture. And she found this there [while
on vacation] … So she was a fashionable lady (laughter) …
it's crazy.

Oslo, Norway, 2012

1940s New York

My silk shirt is my grandfather's and I got it from him when
I was 17, which is 30 years ago … it was his favourite brand,
I assume from his thirties, which would be in the 1940s,
New York. I used to wear it a lot in my twenties. Now
it has some little rips in it that I haven't really repaired
yet but I wear it at home because it's a little precious …

Marin City, USA, 2012

Hiking through the generations

This is my grandfather's jacket and I think he bought it when
he was around 40. It is a Bergans. And he wore it when hiking
the mountains. My dad took it after him and wore it when
he was hiking. And then I eventually found it, and I wear
it and use it more [for everyday]. It is not really thick but
it takes a lot of the wind.

   It doesn't look very urban if you pull the straps all in
and ... (laughs). There's huge pockets ... The main pocket
gets all random stuff and I keep my wallet and cell phone
in the bottom one ...

Vancouver, Canada, 2013

Honouring production time

Well this is a knitted cardigan jacket, in wool and it was
knitted by my great grandma. Her name was Sigrid as
well. She's the one that I got my name from. I'm the fourth
generation that's used it. I really like the colours and it's
really high-quality but I think it's been passed down because
we know that she has put so much time into making it.

Oslo, Norway, 2012

Obsolescence and fashion

Since the publication of Vance Packard's *The Waste Makers* in 1960,[6] knowledge of obsolescence has been building as a key way to influence supply and demand by influencing users' perceptions of the continued usefulness of products. Brian Burns puts it like this: 'Planning for durability was no longer a priority. Obsolescence in its earliest form, meaning to wear out, had evolved into the newly discovered use of psychological obsolescence … as a means to influence consumer spending'.[7] This change, which coincided with the growing capacity of factory production of clothing and increasing supply of materials after the restrictions of the war years, marked a shift in the perception of clothes as a durable consumer good with an intrinsic material value, to non-durable consumer goods with novelty and brand value.[8] Indeed, particularly in the saturated fashion markets of industrialised economies where most new clothing is bought as additional or replacement purchases, a tendency towards a short 'service life', with little emphasis on a piece's physical durability, is a seemingly inevitable effect of the mass consumption and production of fashion.[9] In order for the prevailing business model's bottom line to keep showing growth, garments have to become obsolete, at least in psychological terms.

The legacy of psychological obsolescence associated with the fashion sector is found both in growing levels of discarded clothing[10] and where they are not disposed of and additional ones bought, in the increasing numbers of rarely used garments stockpiled in homes. Statistics for the UK reveal that the volume of clothes bought each year is nearly double that which is discarded, suggesting rising rates of ownership and storage.[11] At least some of this consumption of clothing can be seen as essential, to meet the fundamental human need of protection – insulating and shielding the body – though these physical demands are met with low levels of consumption. In the economic period of 'satiation' currently experienced by those of us in the global North, it is using materials and marshalling resources for development of our physic life that is the chief challenge for sustainability.[12] The work of fashion and sustainability has to influence both our outer and inner worlds. Going forward, it will be our actions' effects in and between

both the material and the non-material domains that will be a mark
of their potential, a measure of their power to foster change.

A process of analysing and categorising the different mechanisms
of product obsolescence has been underway for the last 50 years and
can be synthesised within four modes.[13] These are: aesthetic (changing
appearance renders existing products obsolete); social (shifting societal
preferences leads to retirement); technological (changing technology
renders still-functioning products out-dated); and economic (cost
structures promote disuse and replacement rather than maintenance).

In the fashion sector the primary, though not exclusive, tool of
obsolescence is aesthetics, supplemented by shifting social preferences
and cultural conditions. Here a cycle of invention, acceptance and discard
of a continually changing series of temporary modes of appearance is
disseminated and replicated across social groups. The result is familiar:
a procession of changing styles of fashion clothes that cascade from
runway show to high street, to our bodies and then sometimes back into
design concepts for a new collection. The changing styles work within
longer acting trends and index all clothes as part of the fashion system,
as of a time and place. The obsolescence model has been perfected in
the fashion sector and raises a series of deeply challenging questions
about the dynamics of the fashion system and its effects. It also raises
the enticing possibility that fashion's 'perfecting' skills and talents,
its playful creativity, social imagination, its energy and its abilities to
mobilise people fast and en masse, can be redirected to another model.

A provisional exploration of other models, which extend an ethic
of care to both industry and society, can be seen in two design projects
that formed part of the *Local Wisdom* practice-based research. In
MAKE*USE*, Holly McQuillan of Massey University developed five
garment patterns and assembled pieces designed to have simple user-
actionable modifications embedded within. The digital textile print
is also a guide to adaptation, using key symbols, patterns and colours
to aid the user when making changes. Features such as fit, width,
length, sleeve and neckline size and shape are available as simple
alterations. Ways of finishing the garments so that each modification
can be 'unmade' and mended conspicuously, have also been sampled
allowing the garment design to be changed by the user depending
on their changing needs or desires.

MAKE*USE* by Holly McQuillan

And in the project *My Little Black Coat*, JonMaxGoh from Parsons The New School for Design created a piece which features a handcraft process of needle-felting to act as a visual precursor, a suggestion for how future repairs may be enacted. The action of needle-felting darns worn fabric and joins broken seams, giving the garment a life 'script' which already includes repair, hinting at another type of fashion relationship.

Material and garment durability

Durability of garments is pursued in many ways, often, in the first instance, through specifying long lasting and robust materials. Obvious as it is, but perhaps worth stating anyway; a piece's potential physical

My Little Black Coat by JonMaxGoh

longevity depends less on choice of materials alone than on the whole, the constructed object. Here any attempt at durability needs to balance a piece's lifespan across component parts to build a shared, similar longevity of seam, fabric, fastening, facing etc. It means that workmanship should be as durable as, say, the hardworking fabric on a garment's cuffs, hems and knees. It means that a fabric with poor dimensional stability or wash fastness should be matched with low-grade seam construction. Such tactics build an internally consistent product strategy for durability that prevents wasting resources by under-specifying of elements that will soon fail, when other parts of the garment are in good health and conversely over-specifying resource-intensive components when other aspects of the piece are short-lived.

In the case of garments that wear out, that become thread bare and broken, and for those that are discarded because it is cheaper to buy a new item rather than mend an existing one, improving the wear characteristics of materials and construction delivers benefits. Indeed more broadly, knowledge about the strength and wear–ability of materials and the methods of garment construction is valuable and an important way to build empathy for practices of use that follow a garment's creation. But for fashion clothes, many of which already endure physically long past their period of use, putting resources and effort into enhancing the physical durability of seams and fabrics is worth little if it is aesthetics or social preferences – or even changing waistlines – not material robustness that determines a piece's lifespan. Making a garment last is very different to making a long-lasting garment.

As in the stories that highlight the past three chapters, the stories of 'patina of use' demonstrate an attentive relationship with clothes over time. The intricate, practical complexity of durability and on-going use, including garment-based responses to long life, is essential knowledge – and is tested out in practice in a design project *Patina*, that responded to the *Local Wisdom* tales related to long life and enduring use. Taking advantage of the inherent spectrum of lightfastness of natural dyes, a design team from Kolding School of Design created an outfit that records both the passage of time and reflects the intensity of these pieces' exposure to light. Using the changing colour palette and subtle effects made possible by natural dyes, this work features an aesthetic based on the inevitability of transience and marks use as an activity that embraces being in the world.

Patina by Gitte Lægård, Cæcilie Dyrup and Amanda Nygren

The stories of 'patina of use'

With our garments, as with our bodies, the passing of
time leaves its mark. In both domains, our relationship
with these imprints is complex. With clothes, we sometimes
discard pieces because they are ageing, dated, jaded or
worn; at other times we buy vintage or pre-distressed
pieces, coveting that which looks old. Yet too often these
overlook the power and pleasure of marking the passing
of time as it is recorded in our clothes; forging of memories,
learning through doing, evolution of appearance.

Back-mending

I have a huge mending pile that is sort of completed and added to at a rate that means the pile never goes down. I am not too bad at invisible mending but I also, when it gets beyond [a certain point of wear] I decide that the mend will become a feature and I almost patch with abandon, knowing it will be seen and deciding that it will be … almost advertising the fact that it is mended.

   The shirt … I think the piece was not made for somebody who works so much as I do forward. I'm a weaver, so … I don't know, the front seems to be fine, and it seems also odd, it looks like I've just added the patches for effect but there is actually significant wear under it and I haven't patched where it hasn't needed patching.

Melbourne, Australia, 2013

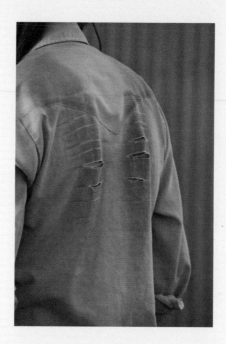

Marks of a tree planter

On this shirt, you can see the pattern on the back, is from
tree planting … It's a Canadian subculture of university
students that work in the summer in the north where they
harvest forest, and they hire people to go and replant the
trees. It has interesting clothing … not style … like you are
working so you wear work clothes, but it's like everything
is re-appropriated. Everybody wears white dress shirts, they
are light and they keep the bugs off and you keep the collar up.
   This shirt started out as a [regular everyday] shirt that I just
wore regularly. And then it got a stain on it, so then I turned
it into a work shirt for tree planting and then I wore it and it
developed this pattern, because you have these straps on your
back and it's really heavy work and you're out there for ten
hours a day. In the rain, in the mud. Then these rips happened,
and that kind of rendered it useless [for tree planting], because
bugs can get in … So then it reversed its role and now I wear
it again for everyday. Dirty and gross, but the rips, are a kind of
a signifier that I tree plant … and that I've also done this really
hard work that I am proud of … Though I wear it not a lot
because [even though] it has been washed tons of times it is just
stained … it just looks like I am dirty, I sort of struggle with it.

Vancouver, Canada, 2013

Second skin tattoo

This used to be jeans. It is a skirt now … [When it was]
trousers, I was at a music festival and I fell down and
broke my leg … My housemate drove me to hospital. They
had to cut the leg [off the jeans] to put me in a cast so they
were completely damaged. I was really bummed out about
it 'cause they were really great jeans and I'm really funny
about jeans … I found them in the charity shop by chance …
So after a few months I turned them into a skirt and I hand
stitched some song lyrics on it. I really wanted to get a tattoo
but I felt that it would be too much. But then I thought I
would just have it on my clothing because it's almost like
that would be there forever and it feels almost like, for me,
getting a tattoo 'cause it will stay on your favourite piece of
clothing. And ever since then I've been hand stitching some
lyrics on my favourite clothing.

London, UK, 2012

Name it!

This is my dad's skiing jacket from the 60s. When he met my
mum they started to ski together with a group of friends, one
was a man called Colin. Colin fell in love with the jacket and
grew jealous. My dad lent it to him for a number of years and
Colin sewed his name onto the collar because he had such an
affinity with it. Eventually it was returned to my dad.

Totnes, UK, 2009

Started with a home sewing machine

I bought these jeans about four and a half years ago. They were raw denim and I basically wore them non-stop for at least eight months before I first washed them. So that would in time bring a contrast between the indigo dyed brought off naturally and where it hadn't as much … So they started out a constant indigo right the way through, and over time the natural rubbing off of the dye, creates contrast between the light and dark … tram tracks [down the outside leg seam] … honeycombs [behind the knee] … whiskers [in the crotch area].

As I continued to wear them every day and travelling overseas through Europe they eventually started to thin out and rip and by the time I got back to Australia I needed to take them in for repairs. Since then I've learned how to sew on my own machines. [My repairing] … has got better over the years. I started with a home sewing machine and now I have about five or six industrial machines, press studs, yeah … You spend so much time wearing them in and getting the nice fades and that sort of thing you don't want to retire them or put them out to pasture. You want to keep repairing them and keep wearing them until they can't take any more.

Melbourne, Australia, 2013

Past ownership is ok

This long top is a recent love affair … it's a jersey thing and
I got it at a recent [clothes] swap two or three months ago
and I wear it like three times a week because it's warm and
it's loose and it's comfortable and it's nice … people like it …
I love the long sleeves. I wear arm warmers a lot and I like
things that are kind of droopy.

   It was really funny when I picked it up and I was like,
'oh what is this thing?' and it's got some snags and signs of
wear from past owners. But I'm alright with that. It's a bit
like with a new relationship … it's had a life before I came
along and I can add to it, hopefully not scars or tears, but
to the next part of its life.

Dublin, Ireland, 2012

Ageing denim

This denim shirt which was originally my brother's, both
brothers' ... I think they both wore it actually, and now
I've got it, pretty much. Or actually, I dug it out, it didn't
really get passed on to me ... Being denim it's pretty durable,
I guess. There's, like, signs of, like, stitching coming away
and things but I really like it.

London, UK, 2010

A true patina

I don't really know how old this is. I suspect it's very old.
It might be 150, 200 years old. This is from Japan. It's silk
and, I mean, just poetically, I want to cry when I see this piece.
This is my favourite piece, if I was only able to have one piece
... It's a bit yin-yang. It's a boat. We're all in a boat. We're all
flowing around in the sea of life. And then there's sort of this
reverse. There's a boat upside-down. And then there's the sky
but is it the sea? ... In fact, I ought to mend this. It's falling
apart. I would want to because I value this so much. I would
want to preserve it in some way and I would insist on carrying
on wearing it, even if it's in threads. And actually if you look
at a lot of what fashion has done for the last thirty years, we
do this thing like we try to make our jeans wear out to acquire
this patina. Why don't we just calm down? And let every
garment we have, have the patina it has?

London, UK, 2010

Denim moustache

These jeans I have in my wardrobe since 1983, for more than 25 years. Levis ... with a red label, that everybody, the connoisseur knows was made in the USA before the production was cut. So 501. It's a blue jean that as it has worn has signs [of wear around the crotch] on it, what in French we call a jean 'moustache' ... Today you can buy your jeans stonewashed, you can buy them already with 'a moustache'. Mine were perfectly blue at the beginning ...

London, UK, 2010

Optimum scuff

I bought these shoes when I was sixteen. It took me a long
time to get them this scuffed. And when I was about a year
into having them and they'd just got to the optimum point,
I came down one morning and my dad said 'I've polished
your shoes for you!' And I was like, 'oh you are having a laugh'.
And I had actually broken my toe – 'cause they're steel toe
[caps] – and I just started kicking lampposts trying to break
them in. Yeah so I'm 37 now, had them since 16 … the longest
relationship I've ever had.

Dublin, Ireland, 2012

Emotionally durable design

Given the role of human behaviour and psychology in determining garment obsolescence, much attention has been paid to the role of emotional mechanisms to construct meaning in order to foster their sustained use. In his book, *Emotionally Durable Design*,[14] Jonathan Chapman contends that products are discarded when they fail to display meaning and that by cultivating an emotional and experiential connection between person and product we can disrupt our dependency on consumption of new goods.

As part of his doctoral research in which he surveyed the product relationships of over 2000 users of domestic electronic products, Chapman developed a six point experiential framework to initiate engagement with emotional durability and design, specifying points of intervention and pathways which offer starting points and lend structure to investigations:[15]

Narrative: Users share a unique personal history with the product;

Detachment: Users feel no emotional connection to the product, have low expectations of it and thus view it favourably because it makes few demands;

Surface: The product ageing well physically and develops a tangible character through this process;

Attachment: Users feel a strong emotional connection to the product;

Enchantment: Users are delighted by a product and the process of discovery of it;

Consciousness: The product is perceived to have free will. It is temperamental and users need to acquire skills to interact with it fully.

In a design response to the stories of *Local Wisdom*, Geoff Pacis from California College of the Arts explores some of these intervention points. He looked to the potential of building narrative and connection through a jacket that 'self-tailors' to the body, courtesy of a lining that moulds to fit and holds the form of a user's torso. Life shapes the garment. Extended use improves its shape. The garment 'learns' about its user through a process of on-going use. Here he attempts to devise a working response to the understanding that in fashion the unit of analysis is so often a garment. But what happens if we change this unit of analysis to the *use of a garment through time*? What if we introduce the dimensions of time and use into garments? What if these become informal pathways of influence in fashion – places that show where the real action is – in our lives?

Bespoke for the masses by Geoff Pacis

Consumer studies show, however, that strategies of emotional durability which work to animate the life of products don't straightforwardly impact consumption patterns and delay disposal. Sian Evans and Tim Cooper note, 'attachment doesn't necessarily lead to lifespan optimising behaviour'.[16] Simply because users have formed a bond with a piece, doesn't mean it will be used or replacement consumption prevented. They go on, 'In cases where such attachment was identified, new products were no less likely to be purchased; attachment merely led to accumulation and storage of seldom-used items'.[17] Chapman himself recognises the limitations of designing for attachment and engagement:

> Although a designer can certainly elicit within users an emotional response to a given object, the explicit nature of the response is beyond the designer's control; the unique assemblage of past experiences that is particular to each user, their cultural background and life journey determines this. Designers cannot craft an experience but only the conditions or levers that might lead to an intended experience. What those required conditions are, however, is still unclear to design.[18]

This is corroborated by research that reveals that those products that defy obsolescence do so in informal or unintentional ways, rarely as a result of design planning[19] and which show that consumers often behave in a way so as to reduce the lifespan of products, with an idiosyncratic approach to maintaining quality.[20] Such insight acts to downplay the potential of the traditional product-centric design process to influence the way in which a product is used, instead emphasising on-going use and durability as contingent on user behaviour. It shows that the most powerful *actant* once again, is not a product, but the user, and that our ideas about durability require a change of approach.

Social relations and interactions

Here I am indebted to the work of anthropologist Karen Tranberg Hansen, who in her research exploring second hand dress in Zambia, is confronted with a similar limitation in the ways in which her field is understood. For Hansen, the problem is that material culture, with its emphasis on socially constructed things or commodities, falls short in explaining the fashion practices awash with social exchanges and relationships that she observed in Zambia. In her analysis she overcomes this by, 'shifting the focus from things to social relations and interactions. With this shift, the point of departure is not the things themselves but rather the strategies within which they are embedded'.[21] She takes Jonathan Friedman's suggestion to approach objects and relations from a different perspective, turning around Arjun Appadurai's now foundational idea of material culture that things have social lives,[22] arguing that her evidence from the streets of Lusaka reveal instead that, 'things do not have social lives. Rather social lives have things'.[23] In so doing, her point of departure becomes people.

Such a shift changes the focus of investigation of durability from the object (with or without its qualities of enchantment and attachment) to the behaviours, habits and material expression of the person using it.

In the case of stories that explicitly articulate use over the long term, such as those which celebrate a worn fabric surface (the stories of 'patina of use') or those with three or more owners ('super long life'), while mending and altering were common, the physical durability of the garment *per se* again appears less critical to the piece's durability than a user's habit of mind fostering long-term use. Durability in fashion is mainly a product of nurture not nature. Its potential, present within most pieces, is uncovered as garments are used. The craft of use becomes contingent on us, as individuals, finding creative opportunity in routinised types of behaviour with existing clothes. In operating within informal pathways of influence to affect what goes on at the large scale.

Wardrobes have been described as representing 'a "philosophy of having" ... both literally and figuratively'[24] yet in the case of the craft of use, a different representation emerges, the wardrobe as a philosophy of being. Insight into such a wardrobe can be found in some of the stories of 'flexible thinking', showcasing openness to what garments and users are and might become.

The stories of 'flexible thinking'

In wearing the same piece over and again but with a fluid attitude of openness and flexibility we can find novelty in familiar garments. The garment itself stays the same, but the rules and roles of wearing it are re-interpreted. Use is intensified; resources are saved; individuality is reclaimed.

Multiple functions take time

This is a top made out of two shirts, two men's shirts. I have
cut it up and made it into a new ladies' top, so half of it is silk
and half of it is polyester. You can totally unbutton the two
halves from each other. It means that you can wash [the two
halves] separately, but it actually means that one side crinkles
much more than the other, so I only have to iron half (laughs).
It had to be made from two shirts that had the same collar
width ... I discovered after I made the other ones what the
criteria is for the next pieces that go together. Which is
complicated (laughs). You [can wear it without the second
half], you can actually unbutton it off and put that over
your head and wear it as a halter-top.

   But I've also found that when I've had multifunctional
pieces I don't really find the second function until I've owned
it for a number of years. It is not something that I necessarily
interchange, weekly. It might be I wear it one way for a year
or two and then I discover how the other way now works.
That sort of helps the longevity of a piece that might not
be immediately apparent.

Melbourne, Australia, 2013

Upside-down

This is a cashmere sweater that I got at Goodwill and it's a large men's sweater. It's a very boxy, basic shape but it's large enough that if you turn it upside-down, your shoulders go – well, with a little bit of a tear – through the v-neck and then it fits on your waist. And so the wide bottom becomes a cowl neck that can be widened to almost be a shrug around the shoulders or closed together and wrapped around and tucked in, which is my favourite way to wear it.

Marin City, USA, 2012

Wear to wear out

At the moment I just wear [this dress] for special occasions
but I once met a woman who was in her 80s and who wore
eveningwear all the time. She'd made a decision years before
not to buy any new clothes and to wear everything until
it wore out. She'd worn her way through her wardrobe and
had got to her eveningwear. So when I'm in my 80s it's going
to be this dress.

Totnes, UK, 2009

No cutting, no sewing, reversible

This [top] is from Mexico and this was made by artisans there. What I love about this is, well firstly, it's gorgeous, it's made with natural dyes, it's straight off the loom, no cutting, no sewing and slits for [arm]holes. I wear it both ways [reversing it]. So if I'm in the mood for something more subdued I'll wear it this way but it's equally as beautiful inside-out. It also keeps me really cool, there's something about this cut that really works.

Marin City, USA, 2012

Hanging ends

This [sweater] is something I made … I had amassed these
various colours and I thought I'll make an entire sweater,
like a camouflage but not. Normally the ends get worked
in nicely and typically it would be showing the smooth side
and be all neat but I decided to keep it with the ends hanging.
I was on the commuter bus one morning wearing it and this
very nicely-dressed gentleman said to me (whispers) 'you've
put your sweater on inside-out!' and I said 'oh no, it's ok'
and he turned all red. I wear it both ways.

Marin City, USA, 2012

Guernsey knit

My grandma just gave me this [pullover] – hand-knitted
Guernsey which she made for me, took her a year and a half.
It's got my initials in the back and she's not got great eye-sight
so knitting fine in dark blue is really difficult so it's a labour
of love. And we, kind of, talked about what the design was
going to be like … And you'd have a different pattern on the
yoke [compared with the main body of the jumper] and you'd
have a different pattern for your village so if you were washed
overboard on your ship and you swept up on a beach they'd
know where to send your body back. This is how they'd tell,
the different patterns. And it's made to be reversible so that
you won't wear these out and you have the pattern at the
top because the bottoms one wears through and that can
be quickly re-knitted in plain knit but the tops are the
complicated bit.

London, UK, 2011

Usership

The evidence of the *Local Wisdom* stories supports the view that durability is an outcome and not an aim of using products. A point underscored by durability's non-linear relationship with user satisfaction: while lack of durability of products is a source of dissatisfaction to consumers, neither is perpetual durability valued, 'a lifespan considered reasonable is a prerequisite for satisfaction, but does not ensure it'.[25] Thus product life extension becomes a nested system within a bigger system of skills, competences, garment-related doings and beings. Here durability of a garment's materiality – its fabrics, construction and design – is associated with agency and capabilities.

Walter Stahel describes this expanded view of durability as 'user-ship',[26] that is something which emanates from performance rather than products. Evoking ideas of *usership* as distinct to *ownership* moves the durability debate away from a product-centric business focus and back to a debate of wider society; reflecting the tacit understanding we have of durability as a function of behaviour related to material objects. Like much within ideas and practices of the craft of use, this is a major challenge, for we are largely 'locked in' to fashion conventions, habits, social norms and industry structures which reflect a vision of ourselves as consumptive individuals, not as users. But if we stray outside these conventions and structures (taking Gary Snyder's advice – see Chapter 2), then a different role for design practices, including those focused on durability, emerges. Here the aim is to foster and amplify the skills, habits of mind and abilities of users to create and engage with fashion from within a context of satisfaction and resourcefulness. This fashion-ability, 'craft of use' or 'clothing competence'[27] is a set of skills, ideas and identifiable practices which are conducive to promoting the satisfying use of garments and to the creation of fluid appearance in dress appropriate to both time and place that is expressed in a fashion 'moment'.

It is to competencies that we need to turn to promote the extended, iterative use of garments – a theme that is explored more in the following chapter. It is in this territory of people, capabilities and skills that fashion as a process has potential to bolster durability and find a new format in resource scarce and climate changed times. This raises the prospect of a subtle but nonetheless profound change, that we may start to value garments not just for what they are now; but for what they and us together might become.

6
Capabilities and Agency

The Stories of Shared Use, Mending and Action Tools

To paraphrase Nobel Prize winning economist Amartya Sen in the context of this book: just because you own it, doesn't mean you know how to use it.[1] Possession doesn't lead directly to understanding, or to the ability and freedom to act. Instead, satisfaction flows from what we succeed in being and doing with the garments we have available to us. It is a dynamic relationship between what could be done and what we actually know how to do and be.

The expansion in rates of production and consumption of goods like fashion without a corresponding growth in our self-knowledge, skills and competence threatens us with impoverishment of human and natural systems. A different, more reflexive understanding can be nurtured by the untaming, attentive, moderating influence and pleasure of the craft of use. Its promise is rooted in building not just a set of garments and fashion possibilities but of building receptivity in the mind to fashion that depends on what we are and do as much as what we have; to the idea that, for advantage and satisfaction, we need not continuously set new record levels of consumption.

Capabilities

The capabilities approach to evaluating well-being developed by Amartya Sen shifts the focus of attention away from goods to what goods enable human beings to achieve. He describes this as contingent on 'functionings', that is on what we do with products, skills, thoughts, linked with the personal resources of an individual. Ownership of a commodity gives us little information about how well a life is going. Possession doesn't necessarily equate with satisfaction. For Sen, the value of something like a garment to the well-being of individuals, and beyond that, of communities and ecosystems, depends on our ability to convert it into worthwhile functionings, into valuable outcomes and ways of being in the world.[2] This is where satisfaction

– and sustainability – emerges. It flows from converting what we have through what we are and do into a life we value, not from maximising consumption.

Capabilities brings to the fore the idea that satisfying fashion provision and expression is only partly dependent on the market. It is, however, fully dependent on the webs of relationships between garments and our beings and doings. Sustainability arises from maintaining and developing these relations, not the goods alone. It is relational not transactional; it is found in the connections between the elements, not in the production of commodities and their exchange. That sustainability wells up from relations, puts the things we do when we tend and use garments, in all of their kooky normality, at the heart of the matter. It makes them fully radical, for they are the quintessential relational flows between industry and the world and its people. They reveal what folks and fashion together are capable of.

It seems that folks in conjunction with fashion are capable of a great many things. In the tales gathered from the public as part of the research project that feeds this book, those assembled under 'shared use' reveal some of this great relational assortment. An informal sharing economy has long existed with clothing, the same garment worn by different siblings and friends, passed around, passed down, and often, valued all the more for it. They illustrate a relationship that builds satisfaction from interdependence, rather than the shorter-lasting effects of individualistic accumulation. Some of its logistics, informal rules and politics are fairly well-established, but perhaps above all with shared garments it is the relationships between the people doing the sharing that are most explicit. Shared use reveals relational sustainability, a fusion of human actions and material effects. It also shows users as competent practitioners who, 'avail themselves of the requisite services, possess and command the capacity to manipulate the appropriate tools and devote a suitable level of attention to the practice'.[3]

The stories of 'shared use'

Sharing clothes saves resources if it means fewer pieces
are bought and we meet a need for novelty without an
expansive, ever changing wardrobe. For garments to have
multiple users, fit matters; but they also have to be shared
with the right people. Sharing works when a bond and
joint identity is reinforced by common use; when a memory
is re-lived; and when access is gained not just to more
and different pieces but also to the values, taste and
sensibilities of the owner.

Twin-blazer

This is a blazer that I got when my twin-sister and I were
travelling through Southeast Asia on our first travels together,
our first trip overseas alone. And there was a place there
that you can go and get anything made.

 I've always quite liked the shapes of blazers but there they
have such outrageous fabrics! And I really liked the magical
dragon fabric that I found, actually we both really liked it.
So I got this made, and we've actually ended up sharing it …
it's probably … [passed between us] seven or eight times. She
is almost as tall as me … it is like the twin-blazer. And it's also
just the most ridiculous party blazer as well (laughs). As soon
as you put it on, it just sets the tone for the whole evening.

Wellington, New Zealand, 2013

Loot

It's a translucent rubber raincoat. I was in Venice, the real
Venice, not Venice Beach, for the first time with the man
in my life. This is about 10–15 years ago. We were out
separately, it was the first morning I was there out exploring
shops and saw this in a little shop and I thought, it's exactly
the kind of thing that he would buy, but I didn't have money
and I just thought yeah, he would buy that and I like it too.

So I get to the hotel and he'd been back with a bunch of
shopping bags but he'd gone out again and there's the raincoat.
He bought it for himself ... but we share it. I can wear it, he'll
forget about it. We don't live in the same place, so he'll see me
wearing it and go 'isn't that my coat?!' and so it goes back and
forth. He travels a lot and so [while he's away], I loot. I had a
cashmere sweater that was oversized. He always wants it when
I'm wearing it and I always feel I need it, so when he's not
looking I take it back.

Marin City, USA, 2012

She still says, 'that's my dress!'

Daughter: When I go to university I take all my clothes with
me as when I come back the ones I've left behind no longer
remain – they're either in my sister or my mum's wardrobes.
As soon as I unpack they rifle through and seize upon stuff
they like.

Mother: I can justify the expense of a garment because
I know that it will get worn plenty, even if it's not by me.

Bollington, UK, 2009

Pocket politics

This is a traditional ski jacket that I bought second hand. We use it in the family, me and my seventeen-year-old daughter ... when she uses it I find all her things in the pockets ... some notes from school, letters, tampons. Today I found her bracelet.

I feel like I have to empty [the pockets] to begin a new day. But I take [the contents] out only if I notice them while I'm still at home. It's a little bit private I think ... because they belong to her.

Oslo, Norway, 2012

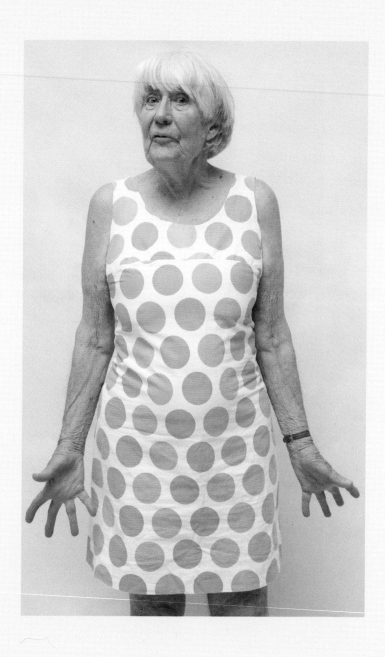

The dress from Antibes

Mother: The people who lived next door gave me this dress
from Antibes which they had worn there over many seasons
and they said I could have it for our holiday. A great success.
And, I can't think how many more years I wore it …

Daughter 1: I am one of three sisters and we were very keen
to wear this dress and have shared it since we were old enough
to have a grown up figure … a period of about forty years.

Daughter 2: So this dress has been going for a long time!
It's a sundress, it's worn really on very joyous and special
occasions so, for example, we have photographs of one
or other of us wearing it … for example, my middle sister
wore it at my mother's seventieth birthday party.

Daughter 1: There's a certain amount of jealousy between me and my middle sister, and she's always asking if she can 'have a go' with the dress for our summer holidays. We often go away together in the summer and the dress always comes with us. And now, almost every holiday I've been on, I think, to a warm place the dress has come out and been worn.

Mother: We say, 'Who's got the dress this year?', when they want it. And in the beginning I had sole possession of it.

Daughter 2: Well yeah, because we were too young to wear it.

Mother: Well, yes but it soon came the time …

Daughter 2: And now there's another generation coming up [our children], who have got their eye on that dress.

London, UK, 2010

Size doesn't matter

This shirt belonged to my friend and flatmate who moved to
Sydney about three years ago and he's about 5'5" or 5'6" maybe
but we shared clothes even though he'd be small and skinny.
I'm about 6'3" … the sleeves [of the shirt] are a bit short but
I wear them rolled up so you wouldn't notice but the rest of
it fits fine. And then the jacket is my dad's … part of a suit
that he wore. He'd be a bit smaller than me as well. I think
he was around 5'11" or that.

Dublin, Ireland, 2012

Colour connections

This pink silk shirt was given to me by one of my closest friends who I've known since I was eleven … I think one of the things I like most about it is it's a bright, coral pink and the girl who gave it to me has a tendency to wear one colour head to toe which I am completely in awe of because I can't […] I seem to really struggle to wear any colours so, it's kind of, it's like a window to a world which I really aspire to because I have so much respect for people that wear colour because they look like they're so much fun. And so I think a little bit of her and her attitude to dressing has come through, through that with me. I think, one of the other good things about it is I wear it in lots and lots of different contexts and I always feel great in it, partly because it is so colourful. But it's really beginning to show the signs of where I wear it. It's got biro on it from where I wear it at work and then kind of a bit of suntan cream here and there from where I've worn it on holiday and also a big red wine stain which is where my flatmate wore it. So it's beginning to show the marks, I think, of quite a few lives.

London, UK, 2011

Productive use of our human powers

Tales like those of 'shared use' display some of the ways in which resources, in combination with what we do with them, can provide us fashion satisfaction. Perhaps they might trigger recognition in us of similar garments we have access to, of similar things we are already doing. Maybe something as simple as our telling and retelling of such tales might build momentum around these practices and hence cultivate our appetites for fashion experiences drawn from lively use of what we already have. The stories of the craft of use brim over with confidence, action, solidarity, freedom of thought and independent choices. Such characteristics are fundamental to the being (as distinct to the having) mode of existence as set out by psychologist and philosopher Erich Fromm. He defined the being mode not as busyness but as 'the productive use of our human powers',[4] that is a mode of living described by an 'aliveness and authentic relatedness to the world'.[5]

Fashion experiences that are alive with authentic relatedness to the broader world – with our relationships with others – are the stuff of change. I want nothing more. Many craft of use practices twinkle with Fromm's productive authenticity. Those of 'shared use' directly exemplify relatedness beyond lone individuals and perhaps go some way towards reminding us of our state of interdependency with the broader world. In his charming lyrical style Aldo Leopold reminds us of this web of connections when he says, 'We fancy that industry supports us, forgetting what supports industry'.[6] And courtesy of a connectedness to things beyond our immediate selves, experienced directly perhaps through the practices of using fashion; we grow, renew ourselves, give to others, enjoy friendships, create identities, transcend our own egos, and for this in turn to soften our desire for more things external to us that depend on material goods. We are alive and connected to the world.

In one of the design projects that accompanied the gathering of stories of garment use, elements of garments – specifically pockets – became a focus of growth and renewal to transform the whole piece and with it maybe even the receptivity of the user to a different experience of fashion novelty. Many times stories from the public suggest that it is the details and components of garments

that hold the key to satisfying use. What if our search for satisfaction –
so often the motivation behind a new round of consumption of whole
fashion pieces – is channelled through uncovering and noticing the
details instead?

In two linked projects, Tara Baoth Mooney, from London College
of Fashion, explored the multiple relationships we have with pockets,
physically, psychically, emotionally, historically. In *Domain for The
Hands*, garments' existing pockets were scrutinised and where needed,
they were extended, altered and repaired to suit the hand and wishes
of the user. The generous, bespoke pocket that resulted, then becomes
a symbol and a challenge, inserted in a garment and in the mind of
the user, for on-going use. Her work also included *Pocket On The Go*,
external pockets slung on belts to be worn over and under clothes.
Here the capacity of pockets to make our garments work in practice
and to, literally, hold our hands, our memories and things, are extended
to other outfits, offering the prospect of not just registering a different
fashion experience, but producing it.

Pocket On The Go by Tara Baoth Mooney

Grooming Tools by Kate Fletcher and Katelyn Toth-Fejel

Another craft of use design, *Grooming Tools*, wondered about objects and techniques that are used to tend and take care of garments keeping them in 'use condition'. Occasionally these methods are geared towards removing all marks and signs of wear in a garment, to restore it as new (and remind me of my paternal grandmother, Ethel and her mangle, pressing cloth and starch). More often however the tools and techniques of grooming operate with the grain of wear and tear, gentling it, responding to it, accepting it. They invoke bodily gestures, the stroking movements of the flat of our hands over a garment, smoothing its surface; the radial, downward motion of a lint roller over the body of a coat; the snapping flick of our wrists as we rid wet laundry of its creases.

The combs, brushes, rollers, hangers, clothes pegs, mending tape and powder, haberdasher's notions together with the hands that use them, work to maintain a garment through life and time. As we de-pill a sweater, dislodge mud caked on the legs of jeans with a stiff brush, hold a temporary turn up with a stitch, strengthen a sagging button hole with a press stud, there is no question that we are attentive and full of care. These rituals become threaded through our days and years and are part of garments' changingness (see Chapter 3, Matter in Motion). The clothes' brush we keep next to our hairbrush. The cedar blocks and lavender bags we tuck between folded items. Our bodies and our minds attune use as a performance for the future.

Commitment strategies

The future needs our attention. Indeed ideas of sustainability are infused with the rights and provision for future generations.[7] But committing to the future with garments and their tools, as in all aspects of life, is difficult and imprecise. The future often feels distant, abstract, hard to factor into decisions. We may, especially if we are young, feel a sense of indestructibility, unsure if or how a faraway future would affect us and how to account for it. Certainly it is hard to look to the long-term and build capacity now to undertake a continuous task. It seems almost impossible to elect not to buy a garment today in order to maintain planetary systems within safe boundaries for future generations. Contemporary consumer societies are characterised by priorities and stimulation that favour short-term interests over long-term ones (see

Chapter 2). But societies are also studded with examples of strategies and technologies that work to counter these effects and help us commit to others and the future, motivated by pursuit of well-being. The critical realisation is that a satisfying life is found in a balance and relationships, not in immediate individualised consumption: 'Well-being is more than having more. It is a balance between our needs and those of others, on whose good will and approbation our well-being depends'.[8]

In his rich and wonderful book *The Challenge of Affluence*, economic historian Avner Offer explores mechanisms and devices of commitment that provide guidance about the right choices to make, devices that, 'underpin the capacity to undertake a sustained task'.[9] Strategies of commitment aid us to sacrifice something now for the sake of something better later; they help us forgo the immediate demands of isolated individuals in order to benefit long-term, shared societal objectives. It seems that they are essential to the work of fashion and sustainability. They act to redirect the observation that: 'People have chosen to invest more directly in themselves and less in commitment to others and the next generation'.[10]

History tells us that commitment strategies emerge in the light of particular needs, function well and then wane. Avner Offer notes that their mechanisms of influence are intrinsic and social. Intrinsic commitment is implemented traditionally through things like, personal rules, self-control and prudence. More recently strategies like mindfulness and now, perhaps, the craft of use add to these things. Social methods of commitment rely on third parties for enforcement, through price or contracts which establish certain behaviours. Together they foster social and psychic awareness of the satisfaction that flows from pacing short-term arousal for the benefit of long-term security.

It's a colossal task. Present-day patterns of consumption take place against a changing landscape in which cheap prices, widespread availability of products, increasing intensity and frequency of advertising and social media increasingly render our will to resist (and the strength of any commitment devices we may have) inadequate. As Offer states: 'Knowledge of how to speed the availability of reward has outdistanced knowledge about how to delay it'.[11] Indeed commitment strategies that worked in the past to pace fashion choices seem outmoded. They feel dusty, stuffy, of a different moral or economic era in the light of current fashion priorities. Today the high price of fashion, once an effective deterrent to increasing consumption, has now been overtaken completely by the ubiquitous availability of low price clothes. And values like parsimony and thriftiness, winning qualities and aptitudes in the resource-rationed war years, today seem powerless and stricken in light of the largesse and immediacy of fast fashion shopping.

Yet Avner Offer sees that our capacity for commitment can be trained and strengthened 'like a muscle', including through regular training, a process of social learning and education.[12] We need to evolve new commitment strategies equal to the challenge of our times. Practise a device-like mindfulness or the craft of use and it lays down webs of connections and moments of understanding, social interactions based on different types of fashion experience. Practise a disruptive strategy like the craft of use and we create a moment for different ideas about fashion provision and expression to emerge, ones which attest to a responsibility for a broader whole and a commitment to the future. Of the many stories gathered from the public in the course of the research that feeds this book, those collected under the title 'mending' most obviously lay bare an already-existing receptivity to committing to the future. 'Mending is minding', as one of the participants states so beautifully (see the tale of *Mending and minding*, p.247), a practical mind-state of taking care of others, of ourselves, our things, and the fashion industry, through time.

The stories of 'mending'

To repair a garment and keep it in active service is to practise the skill of usership (see Chapter 5). It calls upon human senses to diagnose what needs to be done and the right emotional tone to carry it through. Stitching, darning, patching and remodelling oversee a subtle shift in the power relations associated with garments: for the work of mending, unlike the world of production, is about people not machines.

Repair blow-out

I used to pattern make on the floor and so I'd wear through
my jeans really, really fast and also I got these just after I had
my son … so I was crawling around on my knees a lot and
so I wore out all my knees. I replaced it with denim … and
then that wore through so I thought, 'I need something more
hard wearing'. So I got leather … and added this to the knee.

But because it is so much stronger than the surrounding
area, it then blew out above and the [denim to the] side is
starting to wear out and so then I added some linen.

So I hadn't wore these in a little while because I had lost
a little bit of weight and they didn't fit me at all or they were
really saggy and baggy I had always been meaning to take
them in a bit. So this morning in about two minutes (laughs)
I just zipped up the sides to make them fit me again so that
I would wear them and they wouldn't fall off.

Wellington, New Zealand, 2013

Trim together

This is a tank top that I bought a long time ago, in my early
teenage years and you can see it's well worn, it has some stains.
It's getting very thin. It's kind of unique and it has all these
trims ... I added [the blue] because it started to wear really
thin ... to get holes here in between ... so I used the stitching
as a way to patch it back together and hold everything. You can
see it's growing more holes in between but that was kind of a
way to add something to it and to help hold it back together.

New York, USA, 2013

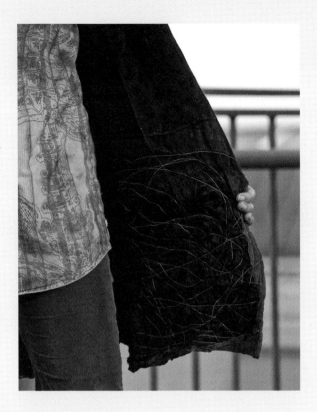

Mending and minding

The cardigan came out of a project by my student Katherine
Soucie. She was taking second hand clothing and re-purposing
them, sort of manipulating them so that they would have
traces of the processes that she likes … the original garment
which was pure black [and] was made by a friend of mine,
Tally. She gave it to me in 1994 … and I wore it for a while
but then it became a little frumpy and I don't know … but
I like the fact that it was kind of two sided and it had some
really nice buttons. So the same designer who made the
shirt was having a mending wall where you [leave items you
want repaired]. So I put this on the wall and she modified it …
At first it was process of like mourning the old one but then
I started imagining it with the clothes I normally wear, and
started to think that, oh yeah, I could wear this … I love the
word mending and it is so close to the word minding, you know,
full of mind of what we do with our clothes.

Vancouver, Canada, 2013

Biggest first

This [cardigan] used to have heaps of holes and it still does
but I've been slowly covering them up, over the years. I didn't
really choose [which holes to mend]. I guess I chose the biggest
ones first, but my idea is that I'll patch them eventually …
I thought of doing knit[ted patches], but it just takes ages!
So I thought, you know 'screw that', (laughs) so I just did
one. For the others I used fabric and then I ran out of this
one type of fabric.

Wellington, New Zealand, 2013

T-patch

I've noticed that all my T-shirts, well not all of them, but many
of them, start tearing here [mid line low front]. And this one
my mom just gave me when I was home and it started tearing
there. So I put a yellow patch on it and continued wearing it.
And this one I think I want to put red on it, I like red and this
avocado green. And here's another one that has started tearing.
The under T-shirt I have on is shredding and I've looked in my
house [at waist height to see what could be causing it] and I've
asked other people … I will keep on adding patches, and it
appears, that's the only place they'll be.

Marin City, USA, 2013

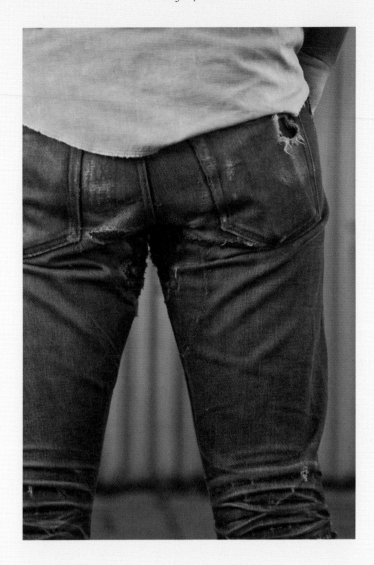

Broken pantaloon

These pants have lived forever. I show people the crotch of
these pants and they're either horrified or really intrigued.
A Thoreau quote originally inspired [them]:

'No man ever stood the lower in my estimation for having
a patch in his clothes; yet I am sure that there is greater anxiety,
commonly, to have fashionable, or at least clean and unpatched
clothes, than to have a sound conscience. But even if the rent is
not mended, perhaps the worst vice betrayed is improvidence.
I sometimes try my acquaintances by such tests as this – Who
could wear a patch, or two extra seams only, over his knee?

Most behave as if they believed that their prospects for life would be ruined if they should do it. It would be easier for them to hobble to town with a broken leg than with a broken pantaloon. Often if an accident happens to a gentleman's legs, they can be mended; but if a similar accident happens to the legs of his pantaloons, there is no help for it; for he considers, not what is truly respectable, but what is respected'.

It is from 'Walden', from the first section of it. And I read that years ago and I started my pants' journey. And I started with a pair of Levi's or whatever I had and then I moved downtown and raw denim was really cool and then I got a pair of raw denim that you can early start a good pair with.

This was my first pair … it was the only pair of pants I took with me tree planting, and I was in northern BC [British Columbia, Canada] for 3 months total and they ripped in the crotch, and there was this huge hole. And I went into town – we were living in the bush, in a tent, but you go into town every week and you have your day off. And you go and get groceries and do laundry. And I found a seamstress, in town … and I was standing there in my underpants as she was mending them. One of the things she had on the go was mending a pair of police officer's pants, which is like fire-proof flame-retardant material and she was, 'I'll just use this'. So then I have the cop pant leg fire-proof patch of material that's mended into the pants.

Well, it's eventually gone through too. And so it's been just this on-going thing, this is the original patch and then it's layered and layered and layered and then it's still going through.

Vancouver, Canada, 2013

Italian loafer

I bought these about three years ago now, at a 'Value Village',
which is a second-hand consignment store. And I got them
for seven dollars. They are Italian leather shoes and as soon
as I saw them on the shelf, I knew that I loved them. Over the
last three years I tried first – because they were quite neglected
– doing some restoration myself … the soles were coming
off … using the wrong kind of stuff, like epoxy, not shoe
glues. So I tried for myself and unsuccessfully for about
six months, I mean, they were put back together, fall apart
and put together.
    Then I decided to take them to the cobbler and I've gone
several times over the last two years to get them repaired.
I think my total investment was something between 150
and 200 dollars for the shoes. A whole new piece [on the inner
toe] was added recently, my girlfriend got them redone for my
birthday. My toe was starting to pop through this hole. Unless
you look up down the ground level, you can't tell that is there
… I like the wear on them. I like the patching …

Vancouver, Canada, 2013

Every possible alteration

These pants are wonderful! They are from a reseller in the
UK, specialising in turn-of-the-century's peasant clothing,
vintage peasant clothing … mostly French farmers clothing
and it's all incredibly patched and worn and sewn with the
dozen different threads and different fabrics and different
colours! And the clasps have been moved and the buttonholes
extended – every possible alteration to continue its life has
been undertaken on this garment.

    Peasant clothing isn't really very common because if
you didn't have that much money you wore it more and
more and patched it until it was completely useless, and
then it was rags for the home. And museums, of course,
have specialised in salvaging and saving the unique and
the beautiful and the luxurious.

New York, USA, 2013

Lost and found

I think everything I am wearing has been passed down
[Though] my scarf I found in a gutter, in front of my house one
day. I needed a scarf, so I went and I washed it. I have had this,
for a good six, seven years, and I've never had any other scarves.
I am not a scarf wearer but I seem to use this one all the time.

I am from South Africa originally and I grew up in a
boarding school there and things always got passed down to
me, so I'd keep on fixing things. So, I do my own hemming
and I have done it all by hand since I was very young. Nobody
taught me to sew. I bought my needle and thread … people
were always fixing things around school. I have got two older
brothers, they would give the stuff they don't wear anymore
and pass it down. Or [my clothes] were [in the] lost and found
[box]. People leave stuff behind and I could fix them and wear
them. If I needed a new jersey or whatever, I would go [to lost
and found] and usually what would happen is those V neck
school jerseys, the V neck comes loose … it starts tearing open
and it doesn't look very good and people would just throw it
down and I would just take a sewing needle and would just sew
that little V up again. A lot of the times, it was all stretched out
in the cuffs and I would just like do the inner cuffs. This jacket,
I lined it myself. This is the second time I lined it … There's
three different panels. The left side is just the original. But
that's coming loose, I need to fix it again.

Vancouver, Canada, 2013

Diagnostic repair

I'm wearing some ripped jeans that I bought at the thrift shop. They started ripping, so I started sewing them myself. I usually don't sew; I've never learned to sew. I really like the fit of the pants that's why I decided to fix them, so that the rest of my leg wasn't showing. But the knee area likes to bend and crease. The reason why it ripped is because the knee starts to put the pressure on the pants … just leaving the knees open allows that flexibility and range of motion.

San Francisco, USA, 2012

Continuous affection

This is a sweater that I [got] from my former wife and it
became a sort of a travelling sweater and it's a funny garment
because you know, she wanted me to stay and it became the
garment in which I've travelled all the world around … and
as it has broken I have mended it somehow. I've replaced the
arms as they've got worn out with these leg warmers and now
mending it more and more and in more places and sometimes
it in the right colour, sometimes not. And I don't really know
why I continuously mend it … a sense that I cannot go back if
you understand how I mean … It's a very dear sweater that just
keeps falling apart and keeps on being mended … it's sort of
a continuous affection. You stitch up holes that perhaps you
should leave to fall apart but you keep on, you keep on stitching
them up, you keep on holding it together somehow. But it is,
I think that's a beautiful part with repair; that you add a certain
attention to that memory of something. You know, you let
things have a second life which speaks totally opposite of
fashion because fashion is never about affection … it should
be ephemeral. Fashion should take you somewhere, it shouldn't
bring you backwards. That's why you buy new garments.
So that's why you dress up before a job interview or something
because you're going to present your future self, your
promising self and not your historical self … Still after all these
years I still think it's a damn good looking sweater with these
arms and it's an ingenious move to make them far too long.

San Francisco, USA, 2011

Mindfulness and agency

Open attention to and awareness of the clothes in our wardrobes, like that which occurs as we mend, offers the prospect of a changed relationship with fashion consumption. It works with a similar mechanism of influence as mindfulness and its attention to the present-moment, to savouring experience, which in turn reduces desire for external pleasures that depend on money and material goods. Psychological studies suggest that a capacity for mindfulness – that is attention to and awareness of internal states and external events in the present moment – results in less emphasis being placed on materialistic values, like image, and greater emphasis on internal aspirations, such as community involvement and personal development, that don't require major material inputs.[13] Furthermore it has been shown that mindfulness reduces the susceptibility to consumerist messages, 'because the receptive attention to internal states promoted by mindfulness may facilitate attunement to deeper needs and desires'.[14] What is more, 'mindfulness may conduce to a greater acceptance of self and one's circumstances: a perception that what one has is sufficient'.[15]

Mindfulness studies raise the prospect, as yet untested, that using fashion pieces with open attention and knowledge might lead us to want what we already have. There is agency here; the capacity for us, as individuals, to act with awareness to shape the fashion system differently. To make heavy use of skills, ideas, attentiveness, community, and scant use of scarce natural resources, and therefore create conditions for, what Juliet Schor calls, 'plentitude'.[16]

For me, the prospect of abundance in fashion is made real through direct involvement of using clothes. With it we supplement rationally derived truths as the basis of all knowledge and decisions about sustainability with subjective experience that reflects life on the ground in a changing world. Here we call out a role for experiment, for play, for composing and re-composing, as a way to better understand the world and our material, social and mental engagement with it. The *Local Wisdom* stories gathered under the theme 'action tools' show such learning, doing and agency. Here profuse use of safety pins, paper clips, knots, an embellishing machine, and even the rain, supplement more conventional mechanisms of wearing garments. The stories tell about untried ideas, of adventures, of going boldly to places not gone before. They are sites of problem diagnosis and solution implementation, a fluid back and forth that is constantly tuning resilience of both us and our garments. They change how we conceive of and relate to fashion. They redefine it in line with the profound ecological reality, stated with such grace by Karen Lifkin that, 'Every level of existence is constituted by relationship and reciprocity'.[17]

The stories of 'action tools'

The tools of use become an extension of our creative
expression and shape our engagement with the world.
Courtesy of simple or sophisticated technology, they
open up alternative pathways of action.

Rip start

Well it all started off at a workshop ... I had recently got an
embellishing machine ... and was excited about the possibilities
as to what you could do with [it]. I started [the dress] in about
2008 from pieces of silk, cotton and velvet, added a bit to it
and then put it away for about two years ... I took it out again
at the beginning of 2011 when I started making and making
and making [using the embellishing machine] and I had
to drape it around a dummy to get the shape of the dress
and I'd add a piece. The great thing about the embellishing
machine [because it doesn't use thread] is that you can rip
[the garment] apart and put more pieces in and rip it apart
and do this, that and the other.

Dublin, Ireland, 2012

Staple, rubber band, paper clip

The jean shorts are originally a pair of my dad's jeans from
about twenty years ago or so and then I turned them into shorts
and since then they've been kind of ripping themselves. I go
dancing in them or adventures or get up to mischief or what
not. So every time I go out I have to spend five-ten minutes
re-stapling, [closing holes with] rubber bands, paperclips
and things. This side's kind of a mess, big knots and things.
So every time it's a new pair of shorts almost when I leave
the house. They rip on their own and then I kind of react
to whatever's happened to them when I get home. Or I'll
even bring a hand full of paperclips when I go out just in
case I need to make some repairs on the go. 'Cause you can't
show off too much skin …

Vancouver, Canada, 2013

Bike–rain–felt

This used to be a really big sweater that my mum gave me when
I was a teenager and a while back my husband borrowed it –
well we used to wear it together, because it was so big, it used
to fit us both. And there was one time he was biking in the rain
in Berlin and he got so warm and so soaked that it felted and
became really, really small. On his body! … [He was cycling]
for probably about a half hour. But it was a warm summer rain.
And because of the heat and the moisture it just shrank …

New York, USA, 2013

Pin for style

The skirt is vintage. I have no idea what era. It's really long and I styled it … it's all pinned, because I thought it was too gaudy.

Vancouver, Canada, 2013

Carry the revolution

This shawl's from Mexico from my great grandmother.
But it's actually what they wore traditionally in Mexico
[in my grandmother's time], high class, middle class, low class,
everybody has a rebozo. And it was passed down to me recently.
It's made with ikat technique, dyed with natural indigo. It's
in perfect condition for being over a hundred years old …
You would wear this in the revolution in Mexico … to carry
your guns or to carry your children. There's a way to tie it –
there's many ways to tie this – to carry things.

New York, USA, 2013

Virtues of the safety pin

The red dress was a little too short off the rack and it already had two nice little layers and I thought it would make sense to buy some fabric from the fabric store and add another one ... to make it longer because it wasn't long enough for me. And the top of the dress, it was a little too low cut, so I just pinned a scarf in it ...

Marin City, USA, 2012

7
Farewell, Good Travels

The Stories of Intensive Use

We are all in this together. Yet too often those of us who are designers and practitioners of industry focus our skills on the objects in front of us and ignore the rest of the system. Throughout this book I have argued for a change in perspective, made essential by the challenge of sustainability, in which fashion embraces the broader world and in so doing makes its whole and the parts more fitting, more resilient, more resourceful.

In these pages I place the context of use at the centre of the idea. And with it, a re-balancing of attention in the fashion sector to favour the practices of garment use as much as those activities that work to create and distribute fashion goods. Such a shift is disruptive and maybe even game changing, for it finds value in a wide spectrum of fashion activity, including that which falls outside the scope of the market. It outlines opportunities for fashion provision and expression separate to the priorities of economic growth. It initiates a long-overdue strategic conversation in fashion about working within natural limits. It does this by exploring the practices of garment use.

The imperative of change

A far-reaching change in the priorities of consumer culture and the singular focus on the market and industry is necessary in order to maintain a 'safe operating space for humanity' within planetary boundaries.[1] In the fashion sector, the need to systemically address questions of growth and the associated continuous increase in rates of consumption of resources is underscored by the realisation that despite substantial efforts to reduce the impact of fashion products, efficiency gains are outpaced by increasing rates of fashion consumption. It is the underlying structures of growth and consumer culture that shape – and limit – the sustainability potential of the fashion sector – structures that the fashion industry is most reluctant to address.

In this book I draw upon examples where foundational structures influencing fashion provision and expression are already different. About half of this book is dedicated to such examples: widely dispersed, ordinary, not founded in industry ideas or a business case. They are the real world ideas, skills and competencies that privilege the practices of *usership*, as distinct to *ownership*, of clothes. Selected from nearly 500 interviews with the public, these examples reference fashion as action, knowledge and human agency driven by priorities of life, by everyday desires and compromises, not just by economic growth. They lift us out of our usual understanding of fashion and sustainability, of what we know.

Key themes of the craft of use

The craft of use is a changed social narrative for fashion, and one of enchantment with what we already own. When we change the stories we tell about the world, old ideas and patterns begin to shift. The tales that feature in this book make fashion ideas that sit outside the market more visible and appraised. They make the implicit knowledge of our practices more explicit, showing us what we can do. They are lots of things. They include: material expertise and deftness; ideas and understanding; spiritedness; ease; human abilities. For me at any rate, they build a sense of wonderment with use – and find succour in the idea that the practices of use we find valuable, *wonderful*, will be picked up and reproduced. In the language and actions of use – in its phrasebooks and glossaries – we find fashion opportunity and satisfaction.

I present the practices of garment use not as a neatly packaged 'how to' list for using things well and with satisfaction, but as rich ground, as compost, in which ideas and practices of use can be cultivated. I hope you will plunge your hands in, dig, sow seed, look for worms. I leave it up to you to care for what grows here, to train it in different directions, to enjoy its blossom, to cross-pollinate its flowers with new ideas, to eat its fruit, share it with others and replant its seed in new and different ground.

The tales of the craft of use contain the beginnings of countless design projects, business initiatives, social ventures, individual actions that show us different opportunities for fashion in a resource scarce, climate changed future. That the context of use gives us a view unlike the usual one perhaps gives us cause to pause, to consider things afresh and even de-automatise our responses so we ask again, and without preconception, about what needs to be done. Those of us involved with industry would do well to acknowledge and learn from it. The context of use tells a story in which industry endures, but is radically changed. It is more focused on others, it is less resource-consumptive, differently configured. It is geared towards qualitative improvement.

The craft of use:

– Explores holistic health of the fashion sector within a changed economic conversation where economies grow less or very differently. Post-growth economics defines and describes economic activity by ecological limits. It switches attention to qualitative development without quantitative growth. The craft of use takes the emphasis off economic markets in order to encourage less consumerist forms of fashion activity to emerge.

– Frames design and use of fashion as part of a single whole. It moves towards a holistic view of the sector that recognises that garments are influenced by forces beyond the control of industry and supply chains. It ties the practices of use in a reciprocal relationship with the practices of garment creation. And with it through real world tending and caring for garments resists attempts to reduce it to simpler parts.

– Casts different people (designers, producers, users), places (industry, homes, chests of drawers) and practices (designing, making, tending, sharing) in new confederations.

– The craft of use recognises that the practices of use are the quintessential relational flows between industry and the world and its people. It recognises that sustainability flows not from elemental compounds, but from synthesis, from what human and non-human *actants* do together.

272 Craft of Use

- The craft of use (i) recognises the influence of consumerist priorities in shaping prevailing fashion ideas and actions, including the building of alternatives; (ii) roams free from the expectations, ambitions and priorities of the 'current condition' in order to exercise its fashion intelligence in a broader field.

- The craft of use is a disruptive technology for fashion, interrupting existing market priorities and value networks. It is charged with different patterns of power and citizen politics that span wider than government.

- The craft of use approaches garments as *matter in motion*, as pieces powerfully influenced by the vectors of time and élan vital that enriches our understanding of the material world. It starts from the realisation that garments are sold as a product, we live them as a process.

- The craft of use necessitates we design with use in mind. That we create with unknown futures, that we consider the design of slack space, loose fit, a shared language in fashion garments, to create pieces in which life can unfold.

- The craft of use fosters attentiveness to garments, 'the paying heed'.

- The craft of use promotes a greater reverence for material objects and a greater reverence for an object's materiality into a larger world of actions, capabilities, stories, ideas.

- The craft of use starts with people.

- The craft of use switches the focus from ownership to usership.

- The craft of use recognises that satisfaction flows from what we succeed in being and doing with what we have available to us.

- The craft of use works as a device to help us commit to others and the future in order to foster our own well-being.

– The craft of use is agential. It shows us ways in which we can reproduce the world differently as individuals and also as a sector. It gives us a glimpse of what happens when system rules and goals change.

– The craft of use is a guide to reimagining our fashion system from the ground up. Its practices are often low-impact and inexpensive. They are low-tech, human-scale and pragmatic. They are influenced by thrift, domestic provisioning, the gift economy, creativity and free thinking. They give satisfaction, stretch our imaginations, finesse our skills of engagement with the material world.

The ideas and the practices of the craft of use are not mine, they never have been. I draw this book to a close with another clutch of them: two practice-based projects that formed part of the *Local Wisdom* design work, the stories of 'intensive use' and a specially commissioned poem. Their knowledge is yours and in this book I return them to you with gratitude and revolutionary heart. I know you will make them flourish.

Grasslands

When we engage with garments in use, we tap into people's lives over time, giving use its context, its place. In her piece, *Grasslands*, that formed part of the design research that accompanied the gathering of stories, Emma Lynas of RMIT has literally connected garment to place through extracting colour from her agricultural grassland (in Victoria, Australia). Eucalyptus leaves, wild thyme, cedar berries and Aleppo pine needles were collected and simmered with strips of hemp to produce a range of summer hues; straw, gold and bronze. Individual threads were pulled from the dyed fabric, passed through the eye of a needle, stitched and embroidered by hand into a sleeveless top.

Grasslands by Emma Lynas

Rice Paper Collars

The desire for novelty, change and a fresh start is one of the enjoyments of life. But through a tangled relationship with market economics novelty becomes a driver of consumption; stimulating dissatisfaction with what we have and creating a desire for something new.

In their layered and formed *Rice Paper Collars*, Lisa Boulton and Karen Byskov from Emily Carr University of Art and Design explored the enjoyment of novelty, without buying something new. Their malleable neckpieces can be remodeled when wet for infinite new specifications and material experience. Everyday objects, a newel post, a mixing bowl, are used as moulds and are the only tools needed to create a fresh look.

Rice Paper Collars by Lisa Boulton and Karen Byskov

Admire and empower

One of the typical insights to emerge from a holistic picture of fashion
as viewed through the context of its use is that resourcefulness and
satisfaction emerge from both creation and use practices combined.
Clothing that is used intensively offers an alternative model of resource
efficiency. Here materials 'spent' in production 'save' materials over
the long-term life of the piece, supplanting, perhaps, the need for
more. Their testimony is both a deeply held appreciation of what
we have and knowledge of what that object empowers us to do.
They show admiration for material goods and simultaneously
seek to connect them with a bigger context of action.

The stories of 'intensive use'

Some garments are worn almost daily. They become both
a backdrop to – and practical facilitator of – our lives and
reflect true resourcefulness. Their features speak of an ethic
of extended, iterative use.

800 days

My wardrobe is from op shops, not vintage but the real deal,
poverty sources (laughs). But I do have a Lanvin ready to wear
jacket on. It's from spring/summer 2006. And I got this from
a friend, who sells second hand luxury brands that he sources
around the world. I bought this when I had a bit of money and
he kept it aside for me thinking that it would be perfect. When
I saw it I was like, 'No I can't afford that, I can't afford that!'
But I chose to buy it because I just connected with it, just the
look of it ... And I honestly don't think I've taken it off. I think
I wear it every day, summer, winter, I just bulk up underneath
and keep warm ... I bought it about three years ago, 2010 ...
and in that time it has probably been on my back 800 to 900
days ... It actually looks like the original pieces that Jeanne
Lanvin designed way back in the 1920s and 30s or so. And
I think that's what drew me to this piece. And that it's black.
I'm always in either black or black.

Melbourne, Australia, 2013

'Blankie'

I call it my 'blankie' and I bring it with me all the time. So I always carry a bag that's too big so that I can have this in the bag ... unless it's a really, really hot day ... And it's kind of a modular garment that you can wear as a little vest or you can wear it around your neck or you can just open it up and literally wrap it around yourself when you're cold. It's made from wool and I've only washed it twice, I've hand washed it in Rose Bubble Bath (laughs) ...

Dublin, Ireland, 2012

Versatility for all seasons

This blue cape / jacket / I don't even know what it is ... you
can put your arms in a number of different holes and make
it [the cape] look and act different ... so I actually use it here
in Vancouver, like three fourths of the year.

Vancouver, Canada, 2013

Useful, handy, intriguing

This cardigan I wear almost every day when it's cold because it's really useful and handy. It belonged to my mother's uncle's wife who died of cancer a few years ago. I got it from her husband … [he] gave me a lot of her clothes. So he said I could just come and pick up stuff like six months after she died, that was like really strange event. I saw her the day before she died and the next time I went to that house there was just a pile of clothes …

I never really thought about her and her relationship to clothes. She was very skinny and pretty but she didn't dress to emphasise that. She wasn't someone I remember as like this amazingly well dressed person. She was very average and it's something I kind of only thought about afterwards … Like this cardigan, the buttons are like this [plain grey] but inside there's a button that's a pearly one. So I don't know if she's changed them to look more simple. Or why the extra button is different.

I actually like it [the cardigan] too much so I put these patches on and I had to sew these up because they were so thin. I don't know how much longer it will last.

London, UK, 2012

Nothing for everything

I brought this shirt. The story is that it's … nothing. It's the
item I bought among other items one day where I started a
job and I needed just some new shirts so you know be clean
and nice and [which would] not be too much work. So I'm just
pulling down several things [in the shop] and this I thought,
'ahhhh, I don't know if I'm going to use it'. But the thing is it's
so basic that I can use it for everything … and I end up using
it for parties, for giving a speech because I sweat so I want
something that's really light. So my main thing is it's so
practical and it's like a nothing thing so I can pop it up,
I can pop it down …

Kolding, Denmark, 2012

Facebook evidence

I had a clothing line and was doing production in Thailand ...
and was helped by a Japanese designer ... we created a kinship.
This is one of the dresses that she designed and I used her
leftover fabrics to help create parts of my collection. So we
did a materials exchange and a cultural exchange ... It's my
favourite dress and I've worn it every other day ... three times
a week; it's a lot of wearing, I've worn the hell out of this ...
a 100 wears a year. I've had it since 2008 and it must have gone
through a hundred washings and it's still alive. Even if you click
on my Facebook account, you can see I am wearing this dress
a lot. It makes time seem really different; when I look back
on photos everything seems to appear in the same era because
I was wearing the same dress: camping trips, trunk shows ...
The clothes are the same despite the fact that time has passed.
I feel no pressure to keep it fresh as I get older. There's a
younger looking picture in the exact same dress and an
older looking picture but what's the difference? It's just my
life, it's just the way my mom did it: same jacket 20 years.
It's almost unusual, so it's almost more special that way.

San Francisco, USA, 2012

When to stop using it

The jacket's my dad's. He passed away six years ago … and
it's been with me [since]. It's unfortunately starting to fall apart.
So I'm kind of getting worried about it. I'm just not sure if I
should keep wearing it … Is this the winter that I need to get a
different coat because I don't want to wreck this one anymore?
It kind of feels like, it sounds silly, … like he's watching over me
when I've got the coat, it's kind of like you've got this cloak …

London, UK, 2012

Traces and impressions of years passed

These are a very plain black pair of boots but they're very special to me … I have been wearing them for the last six-and-a-half years. They're almost dying because I use them for every purpose. I use them as a regular shoe on a regular day to go to work or to go shopping or for going out at night; even for Burning Man festival. I keep on polishing and repairing them. What makes them special for me is that not only that they're comfortable and also that they're black makes them go with everything but they're very similar to a pair of shoes that I remember my grandmother wore when I was a little kid. I was a very girly kid. My mom wasn't really into fashion. She never wore make-up, whereas my grandmother was very fashionable, she had lots of make-up, I was very into that when I was a kid. I used to go their house every weekend and when I was there I'd spend all day going into her wardrobe, trying on this and that my feet were small, so they wouldn't fit properly. There were these black boots, which I would put on the moment I got into their house and of course when I left I had to take them off.

   As time passes by, I realize little by little that my appreciation of certain garments stems from my childhood memories. My grandma had this big wardrobe with all these decades with traces and impressions of years *passed*.

San Francisco, USA, 2012

Craft of Use
by Sabrina Mahfouz written and performed
at the Craft of Use event, April 2014.[2]

> I mean,
> It's capability
> Care
> Agency
> Responsibility
> Use me
> Who's confused?
> Don't be
> It's easy
> The more you buy
> The less you try
> Engage with me
> Not in the shop
> Harsh lights
> Aren't kind
> Use me
> Use that mind
> Create a kind of forever
> A forever now
> Forever is unconsumable
> Unbuyable
> No time for protests?
> Just rest
> Rest and keep your clothing
> Long time loved
> Change it up
> But keep it use it
> Fuse it
> Revolutionary, you are
> We could be
> No guns
> Buttons
> No torture

Cut hems shorter
No split lips
Zips
Bring us to the space of lives
Messy
Dressy
Caress in
Stress in
Using
Tending
Creating
For now
For then
Blend more
Spend less
Master your stuff
Feel the love
Reframe
Up your game
Play
Play your way to
A new way of wearing
A new way of living
Possibilities.

Worser
But slower
We flow into the future
With fashion
Cut from the same cloth as consumerism
And that cloth
Isn't soft
Isn't bright
Isn't tightly woven
With the notions we like
To say to read to write
We believe

Do we believe
Zero fibres to landfill
Is possible?
Why not?
Gok Wan got 100s of shy women
To go naked on TV
And supposedly this made them happy in their lives
So anything must be possible,
Believable,
Right?
9 billion living in sustainability?
Yes, even this.
Through industrial bio technology
Innovative upcycling
Holistic thinking
And all the things I've already said
But mainly
Keep your stuff alive, never dead
Don't worry if Kate Moss is wearing red or mauve
Or purple or blue
Wear the colours that you like –
If they're dyed with tea or blueberry waste
Then even better.
Now let's think of the letter 'L'
The L word – yes you know it,
It's LESS.
Less is certainly best
– of course not within capitalist structures
but as I said earlier
we're just goddam revolutionary round here –
you can make money
without making –
now who's taking notes?
Nurture new narratives
Clarify non-economic interests
Imagine, they do exist!
Models of services

Transparency of processes
Show me
Visually
Who are we?
Who do we want to be?
Surely not the architects of scarcity
We want to be providers
Of plenty
No plastic plenty
Or product plenty
But quality plenty
Creativity plenty
See things differently
3D glasses
red blue gaze onto change
third eye futures
collars up
pockets cut
let's get out of this
pre-planned colour rut
what about dog hair spun jumpers?
There's not much that's too much for us
So let's touch
What we have
To turn reality into a place
That faces fashions
Differently, sustainably
Emotionally, locally
With wisdom
With skills
Not punctuated only by the sounds of tills
But of memories and laughter
Let's try harder
Faster
But with a long time view

Notes and References

Chapter 1

1. The *Local Wisdom* project was initiated in 2009 and received research funding from the Leverhulme Trust between 2012 and 2014 during which time London College of Fashion was joined by project partners: California College of the Arts, San Francisco, USA; Parsons the New School, New York, USA; Design School Kolding, Denmark; Emily Carr University of Art and Design, Vancouver, Canada; RMIT, Melbourne, Australia; and Massey University, Wellington, New Zealand. More information about the project can be found at localwisdom.info

2. Peattie, K. (2010), 'Rethinking Marketing', in T. Cooper (Ed.), *Longer Lasting Products: Alternatives to the Throwaway Society*, Farnham: Gower, 254.

3. Shove, E. and Warde, A. (1998), 'Inconspicuous Consumption: The Sociology of Consumption and the Environment', Lancaster University [online]. Available at: http://www.lancaster.ac.uk/sociology/research/publications/papers/shove-warde-inconspicuous-consumption.pdf (accessed: 24 May 2015).

4. Warren Brown, K., Kasser, T., Ryan, R. M., Linley, P. A. and Orzech, K. (2009), 'When What One Has Is Enough: Mindfulness, Financial Desire Discrepancy, and Subjective Well-being', *Journal of Research in Personality*, 43, 727–736.

5. McKibben, B. (2010), *Eaarth*, New York: St Martin's Griffin, 123.

6. Stern, N. (2007), *The Stern Review: Economics of Climate Change* [online]. Available at: http://webarchive.nationalarchives.gov.uk/+/http://www.hm-treasury.gov. uk/media/3/6/Chapter_1_The_Science_of_Climate_Change.pdf (accessed 31 January 2014); IPCC (2013), *Climate Change 2013*, New York: Cambridge University Press [online]. Available at: http://www.climatechange2013.org/images/report/WG1AR5_ALL_FINAL.pdf (accessed 31 January 2014).

7. Rockström, J., Steffen, W., Noone, K., Persson, Å., Chapin III, F. S., Lambin, E., Lenton, T. M., Scheffer, M., Folke, C., Schellnhuber, H., Nykvist, B., De Wit, C. A., Hughes, T., van der Leeuw, S. Rodhe, H., Sörlin, S., Snyder, P. K., Costanza, R., Svedin, U. Falkenmark, M., Karlberg, L., Corell, R. W., Fabry, V. J., Hansen, J., Walker, B., Liverman, D., Richardson, K., Crutzen, P. and Foley, J. (2009), 'Planetary Boundaries: Exploring the Safe Operating Space for Humanity', *Ecology and Society*, 14(2) [online]. Available at: http://www. ecologyandsociety.org/vol14/iss2/art32/ (accessed 31 January 2014).

8. European Commission (2006), 'Environmental Impacts of Products (EIPRO): Analysis of the Life Cycle Environmental Impacts Related to the Final Consumption of the EU-25', Brussels: European Commission, Joint Research Centre, May [online]. Available at: http://ec.europa.eu/environment/ipp/pdf/eipro_report.pdf (Report); ftp://ftp.jrc.es/pub/EURdoc/22284_EIPRO_Annex_Report.pdf (Annex) (accessed 31 January 2014).

9. AFIRM (2014), 'Selecting Dyes and Chemicals to Minimise Environmental Impacts', Bluesign Presentation at AFIRM RSL Seminar, Shanghai International Convention Centre, Shanghai, China, 27 September 2007 [online]. Available at: http://www.afirm-group.com/presentations/2007/Bluesign%20Presentation%201.pdf (accessed 31 January 2014).

10. Kant, R. (2012), 'Textile Dyeing Industry an Environmental Hazard', *Natural Science*, 4(1), 22–26 [online]. Available at: http://dx.doi.org/10.4236/ns.2012.41004 (accessed 31 January 2014).

11. Chapagain, A. K. and Orr, S. (2008), UK Water Footprint: The Impact of the UK's Food and Fibre Consumption on Global Water Resources [online]. Available at: http://www.waterfootprint.org/Reports/Orr%20and%20Chapagain%202008%20UK%20waterfootprint-vol1.pdf (accessed 31 January 2014).

12. Africa Collect Textiles (2014), About us [online]. Available at: http://africacollecttextiles.com/about-us/ (accessed 12 September 2014).

13. Grose, L. (2015), 'Fashion as Material', in K. Fletcher and M. Tham (Eds.), *Routledge Handbook of Sustainability and Fashion*, Abingdon, Oxon: Routledge, 223–233; Rissanen, T. (2015), 'The Fashion System Through a Lens of Zero-waste Fashion Design', in K. Fletcher and M. Tham (Eds.), *Routledge Handbook of Sustainability and Fashion*, Abingdon, Oxon: Routledge, 201–209.

14. Gardetti, M. A. and Torres, A. (2013), *Sustainability in Fashion and Textiles*, Sheffield: Greenleaf; Parker, L. (2015), 'Fashion Brands and Workers' Rights', in K. Fletcher and

M. Tham (Eds.), *Routledge Handbook of Sustainability and Fashion*, Abingdon, Oxon: Routledge, 210–220.

15. Fletcher, K. (2014), *Sustainable Fashion and Textiles: Design Journeys*, Second Edition, Abingdon, Oxon: Earthscan from Routledge.

16. Brooks, A. (2015), *Clothing Poverty: The Hidden World of Fast Fashion and Second-hand Clothes*, London: Zed; McDonough, W. and Braungart, M. (2013), *Upcycle: Beyond Sustainability, Designing for Abundance*, New York: North Point Press.

17. Sustainable Apparel Coalition (2015), [online]. Available at: http://www.apparelcoalition.org/ (accessed 17 July 2015).

18. Thorpe, A. (2015), 'Economic Growth and the Shape of Sustainable Fashion', in K. Fletcher and M. Tham (Eds.), *Routledge Handbook of Sustainability and Fashion*, Abingdon, Oxon: Routledge, 64–73.

19. Grose, L. (2015), 'Fashion as Material', in K. Fletcher and M. Tham (Eds.), *Routledge Handbook of Sustainability and Fashion*, Abingdon, Oxon: Routledge, 223–233.

20. *Textile Outlook International*, (2015), Trends in World Textile and Clothing Trade, No. 173, 78.

21. Bateson, G. (1972), *Steps Towards an Ecology of the Mind*, Chicago: University of Chicago Press, 495–505.

22. Rockström et al., op cit.

23. Offer, A. (2006), *The Challenge of Affluence*, Oxford: Oxford University Press.

24. Kasser, T. (2002), *The High Price of Materialism*, Cambridge, MA: MIT Press, 72.

25. Offer, op cit, 357.

26. Wapner, P. (2010), 'Sacrifice in an Age of Comfort', in M. Maniates and J. M. Meyer (Eds.), *The Environmental Politics of Sacrifice*, Cambridge, MA: MIT Press, 46.

27. Jackson, T. (2005), 'Live Better by Consuming Less? Is There a "Double Dividend" in Sustainable Consumption?', *Journal of Industrial Ecology*, 9(1–2), 19–36.

28. Lifkin, K. (2010), 'The Sacred and the Profane in the Ecological Politics of Sacrifice', in M. M. Maniates and J. M. Meyer (Eds.), *The Environmental Politics of Sacrifice*, Cambridge, MA: MIT Press, 136.

29. See, for example: Victor, P. (2008), *Managing without Growth: Slower by Design, Not Disaster*, Cheltenham: Edward Elgar Publishing Ltd; Jackson, T. (2011), *Prosperity Without Growth: Economics for a Finite Planet*, London: Earthscan.

30. Daly, H. (1992), *Steady State Economics*, London: Earthscan, xii.

31. Daly, ibid., 182.

32. Daly, ibid., 16.

33. Daly, ibid., 182.

34. Schor, J. (2010), *Plentitude*, New York: Penguin Books, 99.

35. Daly, op cit., 12.

36. Albers, A. (2010), 'On Weaving', in G. Adamson, *The Craft Reader*, London: Berg, 30.

37. Black, A. and Burisch, N. (2010), 'Craft Hard, Die Free: Radical Curatorial Strategies for Craftivism in Unruly Contexts', in G. Adamson, *The Craft Reader*, London: Berg, 610.

38. http://www.kerrydean.co.uk/

39. http://pleasedonotbend.co.uk/

Chapter 2

1. Anson, R. (2010), 'End of the Line for Cheap Clothing?', *Textile Outlook International*, 147: 4–4.

2. Cline, E. (2012), *Overdressed: The Shockingly High Cost of Cheap Fashion*, New York: Penguin, 90.

3. Anson, op cit, 5.

4. Allwood, J. M., Laursen, S. E., Malvido de Rodriguez, C. and Bocken, N. M. P. (2006), *Well Dressed?*, Cambridge: University of Cambridge Institute of Manufacturing, 11.

5. *Textile Outlook International*, (2009), 'Textiles and Clothing: Opportunities for Recycling', 139: 94–113.

6. Pure Profile (2013), *ahm Fashion Exchange* Research conducted in September 2013 on a sample of over 1,250 Australians across the country, Sydney: ahm.

7. Twigger Holroyd, A. (2013), 'Folk Fashion: Amateur Re-Knitting as a Strategy for Sustainability', unpublished PhD thesis, Birmingham City University.

8. Guttari, F. (2008), *The Three Ecologies*, London: Continuum International Publishing.

9. This argument builds on that developed in transportation by Williams, J. (2010), 'Bikes, Sticks, Carrots', in M. Maniates and J. M. Meyer (Eds.), *The Environmental Politics of Sacrifice*, Cambridge, MA: MIT Press, 247–269.

10. Snyder, G. (1990), *The Practice of the Wild*, Berkeley, CA: Counterpoint Press, 190.

11. Farrell, R. (2008), Fashion and Presence, *Nomenus Quarterly*, 3: unpaginated.

12. Snyder, op cit, 191–192.

13. Williams, op cit, 25.

Chapter 3

1. Baker, J. A. (1967), *The Peregrine*, New York: New York Review Books, 19.

2. Till, J. (2009), *Architecture Depends*, Cambridge, MA: MIT Press, 92.

3. Lewis, M. and Conaty, P. (2012), *The Resilience Imperative: Cooperative Transitions to a Steady-state Economy*, Gabriola Island, Canada: New Society Publishers, 304.

4. Bennett, J. (2010), *Vibrant Matter: A Political Ecology of Things*, Durham, NC and London: Duke University Press.

5. Orr, D. (2004), *Earth in Mind: On Education, Environment, and the Human Prospect*, Washington, DC: Island Press, 9.

6. Ehrenfeld, J. (2008), *Sustainability by Design*, New Haven, CT: Yale, 138.

7. Le Guin, U. K. (1997), *Lao Tzu Tao Te Ching*, Boston and London: Shambala, 14.

8. Brand, S. (1994), *How Buildings Learn*, London: Penguin, 71.

9. Brand, ibid., 71.

10. Evans in Till, op cit, 88.

11. Brand, op cit, 55.

12. Till, op cit, 108.

13. Till, op cit, 134.

14. Moggeridge in Brown, T. (2009), *Change by Design*, New York: HarperCollins, 134.

15. Brand, op cit, 127.

16. Brand, op cit, 86.

17. Alexander, C., Ishikawa, S. and Silverstein, M. (1977), *A Pattern Language*, New York: Oxford University Press.

18. Alexander et al., ibid., xvi.

19. Jamie, K. (2005), *Findings*, London: Sort of Books, 109.

20. Smith, J. and Jehlička, P. (2013), 'Quiet Sustainability: Fertile Lessons from Europe's Productive Gardeners', *Journal of Rural Studies*, 32, 148–157.

21. Brown, op cit, 237.

22. Brown, op cit, 206.

23. Sterling, S. (2001), *Sustainable Education: Re-visioning Learning and Change*, Totnes, Devon: Green Books for The Schumacher Society, 15.

24. Bennett, op cit.

25. Latour in Bennett, op cit, 9.

26. Bennett, op cit, 108.

27. Merleau-Ponty, M. (1945), *Phenomenology of Perception*, English Edition 1962, London: Routledge.

Chapter 4

1. WRAP (2012), Valuing Our Clothes: The Evidence Base, 3 [online]. Available at: http://www.wrap.org.uk/clothing (accessed 7 July 2015).

2. *Textile Outlook International*, (2015), World Textile and Apparel Trade and Production Trends: The EU, No. 174, 57.

3. Figures from *Textile Outlook International*, (2015), Trends in World Textile and Clothing Trade, No. 173, 78 adjusted for inflation with global rates from, World Bank (2015), Inflation, Consumer Prices %, [online]. Available from: http://data.worldbank.org/indicator/FP.CPI.TOTL.ZG/countries?display=graph (accessed 7 July 2015).

4. Anson, R. (2015), 'Editorial: US Apparel Retailers Hold on to Their Price Gains after the Cotton Price Hike', *Textile Outlook International*, No 174, May, 4–11; Office for National Statistics (2014), Retail Sales [online]. Available at: http://www.ons.gov.uk/ons/rel/rsi/retail-sales/september-2014/stb-rsi-september-2014.html (accessed 7 July 2015).

5. Schor, J. B. (2002), 'Cleaning the Closet: Towards a New Fashion Ethic', in J. B. Schor and B. Taylor (Eds.), *Sustainable Planet: Solutions for the Twenty-First Century*, Boston: Beacon Press, 55.

6. De Botton, A. (2010), *The Pleasures and Sorrows of Work*, London: Penguin Books, 35.

7. Sennett, R. (2012), *Together*, London: Penguin Books, x.

8. Borgmann, A. (1995), 'The Depth of Design', in R. Buchanan and V. Margolin (Eds.), *Discovering Design: Explorations in Design Studies*, Chicago: University of Chicago Press.

9. Leopold (1992) in Skov, L. (2011), *Entering the Space of the Wardrobe*, Creative Encounters Working Paper No. 58, Copenhagen: Copenhagen Business School.

10. Crawford, M. (2009), *The Case for Working with Your Hands or Why Office Work is Bad for Us and Fixing Things Feels Good*, London: Viking from Penguin Books, 60.

11. Tonkinwise, C. in Dunlop, P. (2011), *Unravelling Design: Fashion, Dressmaking, Ethos*, Queensland: QUT: PhD thesis, 115.

12. Schor, J. (2010), *Plentitude*, New York: Penguin Books, 41.

13. Simpson, P. (2014), 'Global Trends in Fibre Prices, Production and Consumption', *Textile Outlook International*, 172, 50–69.

14. Simpson, ibid., 51.

15. Simpson, ibid., 51.

16. Simpson, ibid., 62.

17. Ehrenfeld, J. A. (2008), *Sustainability by Design*, New Haven, CT: Yale University Press.

18. IWTO (2015), Wool the Natural Fibre [online]. Available at: http://www.iwto.org/wool/the-natural-fibre/ (accessed 7 July 2015); and Woolmark (2012), Properties of Australian Merino Wool [online]. Available at: http://www.woolmark.com/properties-of-merino-wool (accessed 7 July 2015).

19. Alexander, C., Ishikawa, S. and Silverstein, M. (1977), *A Pattern Language*, New York: Oxford University Press.

Chapter 5

1. "The steady-state economy has constant stocks of artefacts and people … The input and output rates are to be equal at low levels so that life expectancy of people and durability of artefacts will be high". Daly, H. (1992), *Steady State Economics*, London: Earthscan, 180.

2. van Hinte, E. (2004), *Eternally Yours: Time in Design*, Rotterdam: 010 Publishers; van Hinte, E. (1997), *Eternally Yours: Visions on Product Endurance*, Rotterdam: 010 Publishers.

3. Breward, C. and Evans, C. (2005), 'Introduction', in C. Breward and C. Evans (Eds.), *Fashion and Modernity*, Oxford: Berg, 2.

4. Finkelstein, J. (1991), *The Fashioned Self*, Oxford: Polity Press, 145.

5. Gronow, J. (1997), *The Sociology of Taste*, London: Routledge, 79.

6. Packard, V. (1960), *The Waste Makers*, New York: D. McKay Co.

7. Burns, B. (2010), 'Re-evaluating Obsolescence and Planning for It', in T. Cooper (Ed.), *Longer Lasting Products: Alternatives to the Throwaway Society*, Farnham: Gower, 43.

8. Leopold in Skov, L. (2011), *Entering the Space of the Wardrobe*, Creative Encounters Working Paper No. 58, Copenhagen: Copenhagen Business School.

9. Stahel, W. (2010), 'Durability, Function and Performance', in T. Cooper (Ed.), *Longer Lasting Products: Alternatives to the Throwaway Society*, Farnham: Gower, 160.

10. Africa Collect Textiles (2014), About Us [online]. Available at: http://africacollecttextiles.com/about-us/ (accessed 12 September 2014).

11. *Textile Outlook International* (2009), Textiles and Clothing: Opportunities for Recycling, 139, June, 100.

12. Offer, A. (2006), *The Challenge of Affluence*, Oxford: Oxford University Press, 28.

13. Burns, op cit, 45.

14. Chapman, J. (2005), *Emotionally Durable Design: Objects, Experiences and Empathy*, London: Earthscan.

15. Chapman, J. (2009), 'Design for (Emotional) Durability', *Design Issues*, 24(4), 33.

16. Evans, S. and Cooper, T. (2010), 'Consumer Influences on Product Lifespans', in T. Cooper (Ed.), *Longer Lasting Products: Alternatives to the Throwaway Society*, Farnham: Gower, 334.

17. Evans and Cooper, ibid., 334.

18. Chapman, J. (2010), 'Subject/Object Relationships and Emotionally Durable Design', in T. Cooper (Ed.), *Longer Lasting Products: Alternatives to the Throwaway Society*, Farnham: Gower, 65.

19. Park, M. (2010), 'Defying Obsolescence', in T. Cooper (Ed.), *Longer Lasting Products: Alternatives to the Throwaway Society*, Farnham: Gower, 81.

20. Evans and Cooper, op cit, 321.

21. Hansen, K. T. (2003), 'Fashioning: Zambian Moments', *Journal of Material Culture*, 8(3), 301.

22. Appadurai, A. (1986). *The Social Life of Things: Commodities in Cultural Perspective*, Cambridge: Cambridge University Press.

23. Friedman, 1991 as cited in Hansen, op cit, 301.

24. Skov, op cit.

25. Mackenzie, D., Cooper, T. and Garnett, K. (2010), 'Can Durability Provide a Strong Marketing Platform?', in T. Cooper (Ed.), *Longer Lasting Products: Alternatives to the Throwaway Society*, Farnham: Gower, 307.

26. Stahel, op cit, 175.

27. Hansen, op cit, 306.

Chapter 6

1. Sen, A. (1999), *Commodities and Capabilities*, Oxford: Oxford University Press, 6.

2. Sen, op cit.

3. Warde, A. (2005), 'Consumption and Theories of Practice', *Journal of Consumer Culture*, 5(2), 145.

4. Fromm, E. (1976), *To Have or To Be*, London: Bloomsbury Academic, 72.

5. Fromm, ibid., 21.

6. Leopold, A. (1949), *A Sand County Almanac*, London: Oxford University Press, 178.

7. Futurity was identified by the Brundtland Report as a key dimension of sustainable development including in its original definition: 'development that meets the needs of the present without compromising the ability of future generations to meet their own needs', WCED (1986), *Our Common Future*, Oxford: Oxford University Press.

8. Offer, A. (2006), *The Challenge of Affluence*, Oxford: Oxford University Press, 372.

9. Offer, ibid., 49.

10. Offer, ibid., 334.

11. Offer, ibid., 60.

12. Offer, ibid., 52.

13. Warren Brown, K., Kasser, T., Ryan, R. M., Linley, P. A. and Orzech, K. (2009), 'When What One has is Enough: Mindfulness, Financial Desire Discrepancy and Subjective Well-being', *Journal of Research in Personality*, 43, 727–736.

14. Warren et al., ibid., 728.

15. Warren et al., ibid., 728.

16. Schor, J. (2010), *Plentitude*, New York: Penguin Books.

17. Lifkin, K. (2010), 'The Sacred and the Profane in the Ecological Politics of Sacrifice', in M. M. Maniates and J. M. Meyer (Eds.), *The Environmental Politics of Sacrifice*, Cambridge, MA: MIT Press, 123.

Chapter 7

1. Rockström, J., Steffen, W., Noone, K., Persson, Å., Chapin III, F. S., Lambin, E., Lenton, T. M., Scheffer, M., Folke, C., Schellnhuber, H., Nykvist, B., De Wit, C. A., Hughes, T., van der Leeuw, S. Rodhe, H., Sörlin, S., Snyder, P. K., Costanza, R., Svedin, U. Falkenmark, M., Karlberg, L., Corell, R. W., Fabry, V. J., Hansen, J., Walker, B., Liverman, D., Richardson, K., Crutzen, P. and Foley, J. (2009), 'Planetary Boundaries: Exploring the Safe Operating Space for Humanity', *Ecology and Society*, 14(2) [online]. Available at: http://www. ecologyandsociety.org/vol14/iss2/art32/ (accessed 31 January 2014).

2. http://www.sabrinamahfouz.com/

Photography Credits

Paul Allister 52b, 90, 106, 187, 199, 203,
214, 278

Fiona Bailey 28, 108, 148, 157, 165, 202,
216, 230

Alex Barton, Monica Buchan-Ng
and Katie Collier 171

Martin Bo Christiansen 79, 119

Jeremy Calhoun 15, 40, 42, 69, 70, 92–3,
126, 128, 178, 191, 200, 247, 250, 252, 254,
261, 263, 280

Jens Christian 39, 65, 96, 109, 127, 155, 282

Namkyu Chun 52c

Kerry Dean 58, 73, 100, 138, 166, 176, 182, 219,
224, 237, 268,

Kate Fletcher 51b, 240

Paige Green 27, 30–1, 37, 52a, 71, 74, 76–7,
84, 95, 97, 110, 112, 125, 133, 134, 150, 153, 159,
163, 167, 175, 179, 188, 190, 215, 217–8, 229, 249,
255–6, 265, 283, 285

Kristin von Hirsch 47–8, 51a, 82, 111, 113,
177, 189, 192, 231

Agnes Lloyd-Platt 118, 120, 195–7,
210, 239, 275

Sean Michael 11, 135, 151–3, 158, 205–7, 232–5

Tim Mitchell 45, 68, 107, 129, 156, 201,
281, 284

Des Moriarty 14, 46, 94, 149, 168, 204,
208, 236, 260, 279

Stefan Rother 26, 41, 44, 49

Mardiana Sani 274

Ellinor Stigle 12, 25, 29, 32, 43, 72, 75, 81,
91, 154, 164, 246, 253, 262, 264

Aliscia Young 38, 66, 169, 174, 228, 245, 248

Illustrations

Danai Tsouloufa 20, 63, 87, 103, 114, 143, 161

Index